HALF OF THESE STATEMENTS ARE TRUE, HALF OF THEM ARE FALSE...

IS *ONE* OF THEM KEEPING YOU FROM BEING HAPPY?

People get less happy as they get older

Believing in God makes people happier

The more often you have sex, the happier you are

Married men derive more happiness from being in love than from success

Women are happier in first marriages than in second marriages

Love is the most important source of happiness

People who live in the country are happier than people who live in the city

College graduates are happier than people less well-educated

Movie stars and other entertainers are less happy than lawyers

Having good friends provides more happiness than being a parent

Homosexuals are less happy than heterosexuals

Money can't buy happiness

Fat people are happier than thin people

An unhappy child is likely to become an unhappy adult

Jonathan L. Freedman

Happy People

What Happiness Is, Who Has It, And Why

BALLANTINE BOOKS • NEW YORK

Library of Congress Catalog Card Number: 77-91477

ISBN 0-345-28535-2

This edition published by arrangement with Harcourt Brace
Jovanovich

Manufactured in the United States of America

First Ballantine Books Edition: March 1980

To Rona

Contents

Acknowledgments

I first became interested in studying happiness while teaching a graduate seminar with Professor Phillip Shaver at Columbia University. As a group, in a total, collaborative effort, we constructed a questionnaire, had it published in *Psychology Today*, and analyzed the results. I am enormously grateful to Phil and to the students—Ngaere Baxter, Thomas Blank, Larry Friedman, Valerie Geller, Chris Olson, Deborah Perlick, Cathy Pullis, Brett Silverstein, and Ilene Staff. Also to Michael Lenauer, a student at New York University, who helped greatly with the statistical analyses, and to Carol Tavris and T. George Harris, our editors at *Psychology Today*.

Bob Liles, the features editor at *Good Housekeeping*, gave me a wonderful opportunity when he asked to help with a survey on happiness in that magazine. This provided an entirely different group of people from those who answered the *Psychology Today* survey. Bob and the others at *Good Housekeeping* were easy to work with, gave me many ideas, and generally helped me much more, I am sure, than I helped them. I thank Bob and the magazine.

The firm of Yankelovich, Skelly and White generously added some questions on happiness to a major survey they were conducting. They provided me with essential data, conducted special analyses for me, and did it all at no cost. I am very grateful for their help.

The people at Harcourt Brace Jovanovich have been wonderfully supportive. I am especially thankful to Tom Stewart, my editor, who gave encouragement, ideas, and criticisms, and mobilized me when I got dis-

Acknowledgments

couraged. Moreover, his editing of the manuscript was better than any author has a right to expect.

Many friends and colleagues helped me with this project. They discussed the topic, offered suggestions and criticism, and proviced anecdotes and ideas. In particular, I would like to thank my good friend Helen Breslauer, a sociologist, who shared her ideas and work on the difficult problem of defining and measuring happiness or satisfaction.

Finally, I want to thank Rona Abramovitch, who listened patiently to my ramblings, who asked all the right questions, told me when things were unclear or inaccurate, and kept me scientifically honest whenever my enthusiasm threatened to run away with me. I am grateful to her for all of this and for the happiness she has brought me.

Introduction

"Happiness is the only sanction of life; where happiness fails, existence remains a mad, lamentable experiment."

—SANTAYANA

For most people happiness is what life is all about. Our goals, aspirations, dreams, and fantasies revolve around happiness. Almost every decision we make is in terms of us has different needs, derives satisfaction from diferything else that is important to us—love, faith, success, friendship, sex, recognition—is a means to the end of achieving happiness. If we thought that any action or behavior or belief led us away from happiness we would do our best to change it. We are not always free to pursue happiness the way we would like, but it is the pursuit that motivates us. Indeed, as Santayana suggests, life has no meaning unless we are able to attain or at least hope to attain some happiness.

This does not mean that we always act selfishly. On the contrary, for most of us the needs, concerns, and happiness of others count a great deal. We are happy when they are happy; unhappy when they are uneveryone devotes himself to seeking physical pleasure, happy. Neither does the search for happiness mean that though it is one source of happiness for most of us; nor that we necessarily avoid all pain and discomfort. Each of us has different needs, derives satisfaction from different sources. Yet we all want happiness and to a large extent we define our lives in terms of whether or not we are happy.

Bishop Whatley said that "Happiness is no laughing

1

matter," and the comment captures perfectly the dual nature of happiness. Surely happiness should be a matter of laughter—you cannot be happy unless there is some joy, humor, laughter in life. But just as surely, happiness as a concept, as a goal, is profoundly serious. While I was doing some of the research for this book, I had two experiences that nicely illustrate the two sides of happiness and people's responses to it. The first involved questionnaires published in *Psychology Today,* and *Good Housekeeping* magazines. The response to these surveys was terrific. Almost one hundred thousand people took the time and energy to answer the questions, cut the answer sheets out of the magazines, and send them back in their own envelopes with their own postage stamps. It is quite a sensation to get bags and bags of mail every day for a month. And long after the deadline had passed, indeed even now two years later, we occasionally get a questionnaire from someone who stumbled across an old issue of the magazine. Moreover, many people included additional comments, sometimes long letters in which they wrote about their attitudes toward happiness, their personal lives and feelings, needs and desires. Clearly, people are very interested in happiness and seem to enjoy talking about it.

My other experience showed the opposite face of people's reactions to happiness. I wanted to have some face-to-face interviews with people in addition to the surveys conducted by mail. Some I did myself and some were done by trained interviewers. I also asked for help from Carolyn Moore, a bright, charming friend who happened to be taking a trip across Canada. I thought she might ask some questions of people she met along the way—an informal kind of survey that I thought would be useful. She was interested in the topic, enthusiastic about doing the interviews, and so readily agreed to give it a try.

A few weeks later she called to say that she was giving up. When she interviewed people in small groups, everyone started joking so there were no serious answers. When she interviewed them alone, the topic be-

serious and emotional and people stopped
. said that asking people the most intimate
.bout their sex lives would have been easier
.ing them whether they were happy and what
.nt them happiness. Everyone thinks about hap-
.ess, but apparently we avoid thinking about it too
seriously.

This book reflects the dual nature of happiness. On
the one hand, I hope that the information about who is
happy and why will be fascinating and enjoyable. The
book should be fun. On the other hand, this is also a
serious book—a scientific document. Although I have
not resisted interpreting the data or adding some of my
own impressions and notions, this is not a collection of
ideas or intuitions. The book is an attempt to present
what we, as social scientists, know about happiness.
Except where I have clearly indicated that I am specu-
lating or guessing, the statements in the book are based
on research done by me and others.

The research has been done by social scientists from
several disciplines—psychologists, sociologists, survey
research experts. It uses interviews done in person,
over the phone, and by way of questionnaires published in magazines. Some of the surveys are random
samples of the population, which systematically select
people who represent all segments of the population,
all ages, economic levels, parts of the country, races,
religions, and so on. Other surveys rely on readers to
return questionnaires, so that those who reply are not
entirely representative of the country. And still others
merely select a small number of people who happen to
be available or nearby. However, overall I think the
results are quite representative of the population because the findings from all of the surveys agree closely
whenever direct comparisons are possible.

There are several major sources of data. First, a survey conducted through *Psychology Today* consisted of
123 questions and received over 52,000 replies; a similar though shorter survey in *Good Housekeeping* magazine received over 40,000 replies, mostly from women;
the firm of Yankelovich, Skelly and White conducted a

random sample face-to-face survey in which 9,562 people were interviewed. I was directly involved in these three surveys and therefore had available all of the relevant data that were collected. In addition, Daniel Yankelovich Incorporated conducted one- to two-hour interviews with 3,522 people between the ages of sixteen and twenty-five and included some questions closely related to happiness. A group of researchers at the University of Michigan Institute for Survey Research have done research on life-satisfaction or the quality of life. I have drawn on this work by Angus Campbell, Philip Converse, Willard Rogers, and by Frank Andrews and Stephen Withey. I have used some older work by Norman Bradburn. Finally, I have relied on all the other research I could find, much of it small-scale studies that were not always primarily concerned with happiness but which seemed relevant. Overall, I had available research based on the responses of well over 100,000 people, though not all of the responses were scored or completely analyzed.

I should note regretfully that one important kind of information is missing even from this large accumulation of data. Although the surveys all included both whites and nonwhites, there are relatively few of the latter and some studies did not ask the person's race. The information we do have suggests that aside from the fact that nonwhites are considerably poorer and slightly less happy than whites, there are no substantial differences in what they perceive as related to happiness or in their general concerns about life. However, we have too little data to be certain of this; to be safe, it would be wise to assume that the statements in this book refer to white Americans. Personally, I believe that the mechanisms involved in happiness are largely the same for all people, but we simply cannot be sure without more data.

With this important exception, we have an enormous amount of data on almost every topic that might be related to happiness. The information comes from disparate sources using somewhat different techniques and different questions. In order to make sense out of it, I have tried to look for consistencies, checking one survey against the others; whenever possible, I have made statements based on more than one study. However, some issues were considered in only one or two studies, and then I was forced to rely on what was available. I have tried to avoid making statements based on small numbers of cases; and when that was all I had, I have tried to make it clear that the results in these instances should be considered suggestive (e.g., much of the work on homosexuals is based on fewer cases than I would have wished, though still a substantial number). In general, I have spent more time discussing findings of which I am quite certain, and less on findings that are our best guess at the moment. However, in all cases, the statements in the book are derived not from my personal intuitions, not from my limited experiences in life or those of people I happen to know, not from some logical or theoretical point of view, not from some philosophical or ethical system, but from the results of the research.

But how can anyone study happiness scientifically?

Many years ago, long beore I thought of studying happiness, I read an article in which a distinguished humanist ridiculed some poor soul who had published a scientific paper on happiness. The scholar, writing with great flair and wit, made fun of the idea of studying something that cannot be measured, be weighed, or seen, and indeed can hardly be defined. He argued that to attempt such a study was demeaning and mean-spirited, that applying the scientific method to happiness detracted from the nobility and humanity of the emotion. (He seems to me to have wanted it both ways; the study cannot be done, he said, and the fact that you have done it is bad.)

Nevertheless, many people feel that it is wrong or impossible or both to study happiness. I sympathize with these feelings, though, obviously, I do not share them. Of course, we do not want to make happiness or any other human emotion seem mechanical and cold. And I agree that if people start walking around trying to measure their own happiness, wondering whether they are a 4 or a 5 today, comparing today's rating with yesterday's and trying to predict tomorrow's, if they compare themselves constantly with the average and worry if they score lower, if people start treating their own happiness in an obsessively self-conscious manner, the result is bound to be unfortunate—lessening their happiness. However, the danger is slight. Already most of us do think about our happiness fairly often—the average is at least once a day—so a few scientists, questionnaires, and books aren't going to change things much. I believe that no area of human life should automatically be closed to study, though we have to be very careful how we do it. And I think that the research on happiness does not dehumanize it or make it mechanical; it does give us some chance to find out something about one of the most important aspects of life.

The question of how to measure happiness is more complicated. We cannot measure it directly with special instruments or fancy electronic devices. Nor can we easily observe whether someone is happy, because it is hard to tell how someone else is feeling. Of course, often we can look at someone and be fairly certain either that he is feeling good at the moment—he is smiling, laughing, acting pleased with himself and the world, and so on—or that he is feeling bad—not smiling, crying, tense, acting put-upon and depressed. But these observations are uncertain. Not everyone who is happy is smiling or laughing; not everyone who is unhappy is crying or scowling. We simply cannot tell with any accuracy just by looking at someone how happy he is; and there is no other way for outsiders to tell. That is probably how it should be. Happiness is a personal feeling, known fully only by the person experiencing it. We do not and should not trust ourselves to decide whether someone else is happy. Since only the person asked can know how happy he or she is, the only way to find out is to ask. That is what we have all done: everyone who has studied happiness has relied on asking people how happy they are and using their answers as a measure of happiness. People may not always tell the truth; they may sometimes distort reality either deliberately or because they are deceiving themselves. But with all its problems, the simple technique of asking is all we have and that is what we shall use.

Let me be clear that by using this method to study happiness we are not turning this precious feeling into numbers and saying that someone is feeling 4.5 points of happiness. We are not taking anyone's happiness temperature and pretending that we have some way of measuring happiness directly and precisely. Rather, we are asking people to tell us how happy they are and we are merely reporting the results, describing which people say they are happy and which say they are not. We are studying happiness by trusting people's responses, and are thus dealing with very subjective but entirely human and personal reactions.

This is not a "how-to" book. It offers no easy ways to find happiness. Alas, the one overwhelming finding of all the research is that there is no easy solution, no foolproof strategy for finding it. I can suggest no religious beliefs, mystical practices (I suppose it helps to have a guardian angel or spirit, but I don't know how to find one), meditative exercises (the TM publicity to the contrary), strange diets, biofeedback procedures, or system of philosophy that will produce happiness. Nor can I propose that the power of positive thinking, looking out for number one, deciding that you and I are OK, becoming your own best friend, or anything of that sort will guarantee happiness. There is no evidence that any of these ideas (many of which have been pushed by popular books) has any substantial effect on happiness for most people.

On the other hand, knowing something about other people's happiness, knowing what is important to them, may give us some perspective on our own lives. What works for one person or even for most people may not work for you. Knowing that many people prefer their steak rare does not guarantee that you will prefer it that way. But at least it raises the possibility if you have never considered it before. By seeing the factors that are related to happiness for others, we may discover some things we have overlooked or underrated. Thus, even though the book offers no easy answers as to how to find happiness, it may conceivably raise issues and provide information that some people will find helpful.

1. Some Questions

Before seeing what others say about happiness, consider some questions about happiness yourself. These questions are based on those that appeared in two national surveys and were used in interviews. I have reworded many questions, added new ones, and removed some that turned out to be less interesting than my research colleagues and I had thought they would be. The purpose of the questionnaires was to find out how happy people are, what aspects of their lives seem to them to be most important to their happiness, what aspects they are most happy with now, and in general what seems to be related to their happiness. We also asked a series of questions about age, place of residence, religion, and so on, to give us some idea who was responding, and to see if there were any relationships between these characteristics and happiness.

Most people think about happiness quite often, but few people spend much time considering the elements that may go into happiness, and that is what these questions try to do. Looking at and, if you wish, answering these questions will provide you with a framework within which to consider the answers others give.

1. *In general*, how happy have you been? (Consider your *overall state of being*, without worrying about specific parts of your life.)
   a. *Over the past few months?* The point of this question is to get at how you are feeling now— not this one day, but over the recent period in your life.
   _____extremely unhappy

_____very unhappy
_____moderately unhappy
_____slightly unhappy
_____neutral
_____slightly happy
_____moderately happy
_____very happy
_____extremely happy

b. *Over the past five years?* This may be difficult, but try to assess your average level of happiness over this period.
_____extremely unhappy
_____very unhappy
_____moderately unhappy
_____slightly unhappy
_____neutral
_____slightly happy
_____moderately happy
_____very happy
_____extremely happy

c. *During your life up to now?* This is the hardest of all, because it is difficult to combine events and feelings from years ago with those of today, but try to assess your whole life. How happy would you say it has been?
_____extremely unhappy
_____very unhappy
_____moderately unhappy
_____slightly unhappy
_____neutral
_____slightly happy
_____moderately happy
_____very happy
_____extremely happy

2. Some people seem to be "good" at being happy; they enjoy life regardless of what is going on, get the most out of everything. Others are the opposite; they never are as happy as they might be. Where do you fall?
_____very good at happiness

_____pretty good at it
_____fair at it
_____poor at it
_____very poor at it

3. Some people seem to have everything that *should* make them happy, but are less happy than you might think they would be. Others are the opposite; they don't have much, but are happier than you might expect. Where do you fall?

_____much happier than might be expected
_____somewhat happier than might be expected
_____about as happy as might be expected
_____somewhat less happy than might be expected
_____much less happy than might be expected

4. What is happiness? I know that you have already answered questions about happiness, but now take a moment to think about what it means. Not what produces happiness, not specific things that bring it, but what it is. Just write it in your own words.

5. Take some time on this one. What three elements of life are most important in producing happiness for you? What is most essential for happiness, what brings it, what makes it impossible if absent? The items on your list can be parts of life that you have (and that bring happiness) or that you don't have (and wish you did).

    a.
    b.
    c.

6. Here are parts of life that other people have considered important to their happiness. Consider each one and decide how important it is to you. Rate each on a five-point scale as follows:

    1. not important
    2. slightly important

      3. somewhat important
      4. moderately important
      5. very important

a. financial situation_____
b. job or occupation_____
c. where you live (community)_____
d. where you live (house or apartment)_____
e. friends, people you see socially and are close to_____
f. romantic relationship in general_____
g. being in love and being loved_____
h. sex life_____
i. marriage_____
j. children, being a parent_____
k. recognition as a person, achievement of any kind_____
l. success in career or other aspect of life_____
m. feeling of accomplishment_____
n. health_____
o. religion (organized)_____
p. religious or other spiritual beliefs_____

7. What gives you happiness now? Taking the parts of life just listed, indicate how much happiness each actually gives you in your life today (or over the past few months). Rate each on a seven-point scale as follows:

      1. makes me very unhappy
      2. makes me moderately unhappy
      3. makes me slightly unhappy
      4. neutral
      5. makes me slightly happy
      6. makes me moderately happy
      7. makes me very happy

If it is not applicable (e.g., you do not have children, do not want children, or are in no position to have children), put an x for not applicable.

a. financial situation_____
b. job or occupation_____
c. where you live (community)_____
d. where you live (house or apartment)_____

e. friends, people you see socially and are close to_____

f. romantic relationship in general_____

g. being in love and being loved_____

h. sex life_____

i. marriage_____

j. children, being a parent_____

k. recognition as a person, achievement of any kind_____

l. success in career or other aspect of life_____

m. feeling of accomplishment_____

n. health_____

o. religion (organized)_____

p. religious or other spiritual beliefs_____

8. How often do you think about happiness, about how happy you are, etc.?

_____at least every day

_____every few days

_____weekly

_____twice a month

_____once a month

_____rarely, if ever

9. How optimistic or pessimistic are you about your life?

_____very optimistic

_____moderately optimistic

_____slightly optimistic

_____neutral

_____slightly pessimistic

_____moderately pessimistic

_____very pessimistic

10. How happy do you think most of your friends are compared to you?

_____much happier

_____somewhat happier

_____about the same

_____somewhat less happy

_____much less happy

Now we consider various aspects of life individually.

11. *Economics*
 a. What effect do you think making more money
  would have on your happiness?
   _____make me much happier
   _____make me somewhat happier
   _____have little effect
   _____make me less happy
 b. If you had enough money so that you did not
  have to work, would you continue in your present job or line of work?
   _____definitely yes
   _____probably yes
   _____yes, but I would change my position in the
    work
   _____probably not
   _____definitely not
   _____not working now so not applicable
 c. If you answered no above, would you: (You
  can pick more than one.)
   _____pursue some other line of work or occu-
    pation
   _____work only part-time at whatever you
    chose
   _____try lots of fields to see which you liked
   _____do nothing for a while and then see
   _____do nothing but play and have a good time
   _____pursue a hobby
   _____other
 d. If you had a lot more money, would you
  change other things in your life, such as where
  you live, whom you live with, what you do with
  your time, etc.? In other words, would more
  money have a big effect on your day-to-day
  life?
   _____yes, I would change many things
   _____yes, but only a few things would change
   _____no, not much would change
 e. In general, how satisfied are you with your job,
  career, or occupation? This refers to the work
  you do, whatever it is, including taking care of

a family, writing poetry, going to school, traditional jobs.

_____very satisfied

_____moderately satisfied

_____slightly satisfied

_____slightly dissatisfied

_____moderately dissatisfied

_____very dissatisfied

f. What do you think about the amount of time you spend on your job or occupation?

_____too much

_____about right

_____too little

g. Do you think your job or occupation allows you to use your talents, skills, and other qualities as fully as possible? In other words, regardless of your actual success, is this a good way for you to be sepnding your time?

_____yes, perfect for me

_____yes, quite good for me

_____OK, but not great

_____no, not very good for me

_____no, terrible for me

h. How important to you are money, material possessions, and the other things that go with wealth? (Not important necessarily in terms of bringing happiness, but in the sense that you care about them and want or need them.)

_____very important

_____moderately important

_____slightly important

_____not very important

_____totally unimportant

12. *Interpersonal Relationships*

a. Do you have a lot of good friends? We all differ somewhat in what we mean by "good friends." This refers to people you feel close to, see often, can count on when you need them. How many do you have? (Exclude relatives.)_____

b. How many relatives do you see often and consider close friends?_____

   c. How many other people, not so close, do you see socially fairly regularly?_____

   d. In general, do you feel that you have as many friends of the various kinds as you would like?
     _____yes
     _____no

   e. Are you in love now?
     _____yes
     _____no

   f. If yes, how does the other person feel?
     _____I love a lot more
     _____I love a little more
     _____we love equally
     _____other loves a little more
     _____other loves a lot more

   g. Do you feel that you have had enough love in your life, from parents, friends, lovers, whomever?
     _____yes, lots of love
     _____yes, but could have used even more
     _____no, had some but could have used a lot more
     _____no, never had much love

   h. How many people have you been in love with? (This refers to romantic, sexual relationships regardless of whether the others returned the love.)_____

13. *Sex Life*

   a. With how many people have you had intimate sexual relations?_____

   b. How frequently do you have sexual relations now?

   c. How frequently do you masturbate now?

d. How do you think other people of your age and sex compare with you in the number of sexual partners they have had?

_____more partners

_____about the same

_____fewer partners

e. How do you think other people of your age and sex compare with you in the frequency of sexual relations?

_____more frequently

_____about the same

_____less frequently

f. How do you think other people your age and sex compare with you in sexual satisfaction in general?

_____I'm more satisfied

_____about the same

_____I'm less satisfied

g. What is your sexual preference?

_____exclusively heterosexual

_____mainly heterosexual

_____bisexual (more or less equal attraction to both sexes)

_____mainly homosexual

_____exclusively homosexual

h. If you are mainly or exclusively heterosexual, have you ever had homosexual experiences? (You can check more than one.)

_____no

_____yes, before puberty (about age 12)

_____yes, during adolescence

_____yes, after age 18

i. If you are mainly or exclusively homosexual, have you ever had heterosexual experiences? (You can check more than one.)

_____no

_____yes, during adolescence

_____yes, after age 20

j. How much do you like sex, regardless of how satisfied with it you happen to be?

_____love it

_____like it moderately
_____like it somewhat
_____neutral
_____dislike it

14. *Marriage*
    a. Are you:
        _____single
        _____married for the first time
        _____married more than once
        _____divorced
        _____widowed
        _____living with someone in a romantic sexual relationship
    b. Are you happy with your current marital state?
        _____yes, just right
        _____yes, but often I wish I were single, married, or whatever
        _____no, unhappy
    c. If you are married, do you think: (check all that apply)
        _____it was a good thing to do
        _____you would do it all over if you had the chance
        _____you would not do it
        _____you want to get divorced
        _____living together would have been better
        _____it was a terrible decision

15. *Children*
    a. If you have children, would you have them again if you had the choice?
        _____yes   _____no
    b. How have they affected your happiness?
        _____contributed greatly
        _____contributed moderately
        _____little effect
        _____reduced moderately
        _____reduced greatly
    c. What are the pluses and minuses of having children?

    d. At what age did your children give you the most happiness (their age, that is)?

16. *Personal growth*
    a. To what extent do you accept yourself as a person, with strengths and weaknesses, good points and bad?
        _____fully
        _____moderately
        _____somewhat
        _____cannot accept myself
    b. To what extent do you like yourself?
        _____great deal
        _____moderately
        _____slightly
        _____dislike slightly
        _____dislike moderately
        _____dislike a great deal
    c. Do you feel you have grown as a person over the past few years?
        _____yes, grown a lot
        _____yes, grown a little
        _____no, not grown much
        _____no, not at all
    d. Are you happy with your accomplishments in life? (These can be anything and need not be recognized by others.)
        _____yes, very happy
        _____yes, moderately happy
        _____slightly happy
        _____slightly unhappy
        _____moderately unhappy
        _____very unhappy

17. *Physical Appearance*
    a. Do you think you are physically attractive?
        _____very much
        _____moderately
        _____slightly
        _____slightly unattractive

___moderately unattractive

___very unattractive

b. What is the worst thing about your appearance?

c. Do you think you attract members of the opposite sex (or same sex if that is the important question)?

___yes, very much

___yes, moderately

___yes, slightly

___no, not much

d. How important is physical appearance to you?

___very

___moderately

___slightly

___not important

e. Are you overweight?

___yes   ___no

f. Are you currently dieting to lose weight or maintain current weight?

___yes   ___no

18. *General Attitudes*

a. How much control do you think you have over the good things that happen to you in life?

___great deal of control

___moderate amount of control

___only a little control

___almost no control

b. How much control do you think you have over the bad things that happen to you?

___great deal of control

___moderate amount of control

___only a little control

___almost no control

c. Do you feel your life has meaning and direction?

___yes, definitely

___yes, moderately

___yes, somewhat

_____no, little or no direction and meaning

d. What pace of life do you prefer?
_____very fast
_____moderately fast
_____not too fast
_____fairly slow
_____very slow

e. Given a choice between peace and quiet and excitement and activity, which would you pick?
_____peace and quiet
_____excitement and activity

f. If you could live anywhere—there were no restrictions of any kind—where would you choose? (Think of a particular place. Also, what kind of place, type of community or area.)

g. If you are not living there now, why not?

19. *Early life*
a. How happy were you as a child (under 12)?
_____extremely happy
_____very happy
_____moderately happy
_____slightly happy
_____neutral
_____slightly unhappy

b. What was your mother's relationship with you?
_____very warm
_____somewhat warm
_____sometimes warm, sometimes not
_____somewhat cold
_____very cold
_____didn't grow up with a mother around

c. What was your father's relationship with you?
_____very warm
_____somewhat warm

_____sometimes warm, sometimes not

_____somewhat cold

_____very cold

_____didn't grow up with a father around

d. To what extent did you feel loved by your parents or whoever raised you?

_____very loved

_____moderately loved

_____slightly loved

_____never sure of their love

_____felt unloved

_____felt very unloved

e. To what extent did you feel they believed in you and supported you?

_____a great deal

_____moderately

_____slightly

_____not much

_____not at all

f. Did you have friends as a child?

_____yes   _____no

Were you popular?

_____yes   _____no

Did you feel liked, respected, accepted by other children?

_____yes   _____no

g. Can you remember any childhood experience or events that had a big impact on you at the time? And do you think they had effects on the rest of your life?

h. Did you have a close friend during childhood (one or more)?

_____yes   _____no

i. Did your parents (or substitutes) get along with each other during your childhood, or was there conflict, fighting, and dissatisfaction?

_____got along very well

_____moderately well

_____fairly well
_____poorly
_____terribly

j. Did they:
_____stay together
_____get divorced or separated?

20. *Adolescence*
   a. How happy were you as an adolescent (12-18)?
   _____extremely happy
   _____very happy
   _____moderately happy
   _____slightly happy
   _____neutral
   _____slightly unhappy
   _____moderately unhappy
   _____very unhappy
   _____extremely unhappy
   b. Did you feel liked, respected, accepted by others of your age?
   _____yes, a great deal
   _____moderately
   _____somewhat
   _____not much
   _____not at all
   c. Did you have a lot of friends?
   _____yes   _____no
   d. Were you popular with members of the opposite sex? Did you date a lot?
   _____yes   _____no
   e. Did your parents love and support you during this period?
   _____yes, a great deal
   _____moderately
   _____somewhat
   _____not much
   _____not at all
   f. Did you fight with them during your adolescence?
   _____yes, a lot

_____somewhat
_____a little
_____not at all

g. Can you remember any experience during adolescence that had a big impact on you at the time? Do you think it has had lasting effects?

h. Was your first sexual experience a good one (i.e. first sexual intercourse)?
_____very good
_____moderately good
_____fair
_____bad
_____very bad

i. In general, did you deal with sex easily, or was it difficult?
_____very easy
_____moderately easy
_____fairly easy
_____fairly difficult
_____moderately difficult
_____very difficult

21. Basic factors that often have important relationships with happiness:
a. what is your age
b. sex
c. family income
d. what level of education do you have?
_____did you finish grade school
_____finished grade school
_____some high school
_____high school graduate
_____some college
_____college graduate
_____some graduate training
_____graduate degree
e. Do you have any physical problems or disabilities?

f. Do you have a drinking or drug problem?

22. If you could share someone else's life for a while, live in their shoes, have their experiences, whose life would you pick? Why?

23. Happiness again.
Now that you have answered or thought about all sorts of things and considered many different aspects of your life, as well as trying to define happiness, answer the original question again:

a. How happy have you been over the past few months?

_____extremely happy
_____very happy
_____moderately happy
_____slightly happy
_____neutral
_____slightly unhappy
_____moderately unhappy
_____very unhappy
_____extremely unhappy

b. What single thing do you think could increase your happiness the most?

c. If you could make one wish (a realistic wish, not eternal life or something like that), what would you wish for?

d. Is there anything I haven't asked that you think is important to happiness?

Now, let's see what others say . . .

2. What Is Happiness?

". . . wanting what you want, getting what you get, and hoping that the two will coincide."
— HOWARD MUMFORD JONES

In the Declaration of Independence, Thomas Jefferson proclaimed that each of us has the right to life and liberty, but only to the pursuit of happiness. He refused to guarantee us something government could not deliver (though that has rarely stopped other politicians). And Jefferson chose his words very carefully. He did not talk about the "search" for happiness, though that is a familiar phrase. "Search" implies that there is something sitting out there somewhere waiting to be found, and that once discovered, it is ours to keep. No, as Jefferson knew, we must pursue happiness because it is elusive, difficult to grasp, and once caught, difficult to hold.

Happiness is not only hard to find, it is difficult even to define. When scientists study something, they are very careful about definitions and measurements. If you want to study obesity, you define it as being heavier than a person should be, or perhaps 15 percent overweight; you agree on what "correct" weight means, and then by weighing and measuring people you can decide if they are obese. We use the same procedure for all sorts of psychological and physical factors. But what do we do with happiness?

One way of finding a definition is to see what various people have offered. As you might expect, thousands of writers and philosophers have suggested definitions of happiness. In style and simplicity they range all the way from ". . . the emotional wholeness and well-being of the personality, produced by activities and relationships which lead to a self-fulfillment appropriate to the age and aptitudes of the individual involved" (F. A. Magoun) to William James's succinct ". . . agreement of a person's inner life with the realities of his outer experience" and Jean Jacques Rousseau's "a good bank account, a good cook, and a good digestion." In a marvelous series of lectures on happiness Howard Mumford Jones mentioned a large number of definitions and suggested that they all boil down to happiness's being ". . . wanting what you want, getting what you get, and hoping the two will coincide." But even this, which he offered somewhat facetiously, is hardly satisfactory. Indeed, Jones concluded that happiness cannot be defined, that it ". . . belongs to that category of words, the meaning of which everybody knows but the definition of which nobody can give."

Perhaps Jones is right, but it is important for us to come to some agreement as to what we are talking about. When we ask people whether they are happy, we must have a general idea what they mean by the word so we can understand their answers, even if we cannot come up with a neat, concise definition. We also need to know whether most people mean the same thing. We therefore asked many people what they mean by happiness. We interviewed people in person and by telephone. Hundreds of others volunteered definitions when they responded to the various surveys on happiness.

From these responses it is clear that people are in considerable agreement as to what they mean by happiness. To begin with, happiness is a good state, one that includes the desirable things in life, that does not include negative, unpleasant, painful events or experiences, and that makes you feel good about yourself and the world in general. Almost everyone thinks that happiness is one of the goals, if not the major goal, of life. However, people differed considerably in the specific terms they used and, to some extent, in their overall views. The responses fall into two groups that emphasize different aspects of happiness.

Happiness as Fun, Excitement, Pleasure

A thirty-four-year-old graphic designer in New York City, married, one child, earning about eighteen thousand a year, says: "Happiness is enjoying myself and having everything go well." A twenty-eight-year-old woman with some postgraduate education is a housewife with two children. To her happiness is "pleasurable experiences." A forty-three-year-old housewife whose husband earns a great deal of money agrees: "Happiness is anything that gives pleasure." A seventy-year-old widow who lives in Monroe, Georgia, says simply: "Happiness is when things are going good, when you're having fun." And a thirty-six-year-old woman, a union organizer in a small town in northern New Hampshire told me that happiness was "having a good time; making just about everything you do a good time."

These people focus on the active enjoyment of life. They use the term pleasure frequently. They do not seem to mean just physical pleasure, though there is much talk of that, but pleasure from all sources—sex, a good meal, a successful tennis match, a "fun" movie, a good party, and so on. Also, these people recognize that one gets pleasure from acts of creativity, helping a friend, being loved, doing something nice for people you love or having them do so for you, and sharing in the success and satisfaction of loved ones. The one clear theme that runs through this view of happiness is that the pleasure and good times, whatever their sources, involve mostly active, dynamic experiences. They derive from something happening to you or to someone else, from some action of yours, from interactions between you and others or the world. The picture of happiness that emerges is lively, arousing, full of motion. According to this view, someone who is happy probably has a faster heartbeat than usual, is moving rather than standing still, going out rather than staying home; reaching out to people and the world rather than retreating into himself, seeking activities and experiences rather than settling for what he has.

Yet these people seem to understand that happiness is not simply pleasure or enjoyment; that pleasures, no matter how many, do not guarantee happiness; that happiness is something more. In *The Analysis of Happiness,* Wladyslaw Tatarkiewicz states this very nicely. "Pleasure stands in more or less the same relationship to happiness as a tree to a park. There can be no park without trees, but trees, however many there may be, do not of themselves make a park." All of those who stress pleasure and excitement also include other phrases such as "being relaxed," "feeling peaceful," and "acceptance."

Happiness as Peace of Mind and Contentment

A twenty-four-year-old musician, married with one child and another on the way, tells us that "happiness is a feeling of self-satisfaction and equilibrium." A thirty-eight-year-old woman with a Ph.D. in biochemistry, a researcher, who is married and has two children, says simply, "Happiness is being satisfied." A twenty-three-year-old man who manages a restaurant says that "happiness is peace of mind. Then you can function physically and mentally without friction and get by without any trouble." Others use terms such as "satisfaction," "ability to cope," "feeling fulfilled." Many people stress self-acceptance. A housewife from Long Island answered that happiness was "feeling content with myself." A forty-year-old man from Vermont thought that it was "being secure in my feelings about myself." And a thirty-three-year-old woman defined happiness as "feeling fulfilled and worthwhile."

This view often focused on the absence of negative feelings and experiences. A thirty-year-old man with a college education and a good job said that happiness was "not being unhappy." A young woman declared it "being free of worries about things I can't control." A twenty-two-year-old student artist, married with a child, said she conceived of happiness as "not having anxiety attacks." And finally, a nine-year-old boy told us that happiness was "when I can do the things I want without having to look for a ride or be home for dinner."

Though these views differ somewhat from each other, they all contrast with the first group of opinions: for this second group, happiness is more peaceful, quiet, passive, and perhaps internal. It involves satisfactions rather than thrills, contentment rather than fun, peace instead of pleasure. It stresses internal harmony, personal lack of conflict, a feeling of having done well or of getting what one wants, a sense of control, and acceptance of both the self and the world.

These different viewpoints—pleasure and peace—are not affected by age. One might expect that younger people would emphasize fun and excitement while older people would say that happiness was more to be found in quiet satisfactions. This is not the case at all. In all our surveys we found no relationship between age and definition of happiness. Many older people talked almost entirely of pleasure, excitement, fun; many younger people totally of peace of mind and self-acceptance. Thus, it is apparently not age but world view or self-concept that determines which definition you favor.

Peace with Pleasure

Among those who gave definitions of happiness, about an equal number stressed each point of view. Enjoyment, fun, and pleasure were mentioned as often as peace of mind, tranquillity, self-acceptance, and contentment. The exact numbers are not especially important because we are not looking for a scientific fact, but rather for an understanding of what most people mean by the term happiness. Nevertheless, it is probably significant that the two sides to the coin come up about equally often.

The various images of happiness ranging from

pleasure and fun to self-acceptance, contentment, and peace of mind do not seem to me to be inconsistent with one another. Indeed, most people included more than one in their definitions of happiness. Even those who strongly stressed a particular view usually mentioned the other as well. Almost everyone seemed to define happiness in both active and passive terms.

Accordingly, it seems that both must be included. You cannot conceive of happiness without pleasures. They do not have to be physical, though most of us would require them; but they must be active pleasures: joy, excitement, and fun. On the other hand, it is equally impossible to conceive of happiness without peace of mind and self-acceptance. You might still enjoy your pleasures, still have fleeting moments of fun and excitement. But even these would not make you happy if you were troubled inwardly. They would not provide the enduring emotional state that most of us think of as happiness.

The active and passive views of happiness are two aspects of the same state, not two different states. Just as trees alone do not make a park, you cannot have much of a park without trees. Eating well, having a great sex life, experiencing continual moments of excitement, thrills, and laughter do not necessarily constitute happiness. Yet it is as hard to imagine happiness without a good portion of these experiences as it is to imagine happiness without peace of mind. The combination produces or is happiness, either alone is not.

Happiness Is an Enduring State

Earlier, I said that happiness is not something that, once found, is permanently with you. Happiness can be pursued; it can be found; but it can also be lost. Yet it should be clear—and this is important—that happiness, as we are considering it in this book, is a relatively long-lasting state, not a momentary feeling. People often say that a particular event or experience made them happy for a moment: "I'm happy we won the game," "I'm happy that the movie turned out to be good," "I'm happy that the rice was not overcooked." It is almost impossible to say whether the feeling produced by a momentary joy is equivalent to the more general state of happiness. We can, however, say that the happiness we are discussing is the more general, longer-lasting kind. We are not trying to decide what makes someone happy at one moment on a given day; we are not trying to collect a list of people's favorite Christmas presents, meals, sexual pleasures, or other satisfactions. Instead, we are dealing with what makes people feel that their lives in general are happy, however gloomy or joyful they may feel this minute. Happiness endures—not for long, perhaps, but for a while.

It is possible, however, that this general state of happiness consists of or derives from the individual moments of happiness. Perhaps if you have many of these moments, you consider yourself happy; perhaps if you have few, you consider yourself unhappy; perhaps happiness is the ratio of good to bad moments. At the end of the book I shall return to this subject. For now, the important point is that we are concerned with happiness as a general state, not as a reaction to a specific, isolated event. We have fairly good agreement as to what this kind of happiness is.

A Matter of Emphasis

As we have seen, people differ in their definitions of happiness: some emphasize active pleasure, some passive contentment. Although most of the people we questioned mentioned both parts of this definition, there were clear differences in emphasis. Those who emphasize pleasure would trade a certain amount of peace for more excitement; they would put up with some negative experiences in exchange for more dynamic, positive ones; they would be willing to suffer a little, endure some frustrations and annoyances, be upset emotionally, if it meant they could have additional moments of joy. They would probably prefer to live in cities rather than small towns, would rather live in a large, boisterous family than quietly alone, would find more happiness in a noisy party than in a quiet country walk. In contrast, others place more importance on inner peace, contentment, feelings of satisfaction and self-acceptance. These people would give up some of the excitement for more peace. And they would probably prefer the quiet satisfactions and contentment of rural or small town life to the louder, more active pleasures of a city.

Despite these differences in emphasis, people generally agree about what they mean by happiness. It is a positive, enduring state that consists of positive feelings about the self and the world and that includes both peace of mind and active pleasures and joy. The differences among people rest not so much in the basic underlying meaning of the concept, as in the particular mixture that produces happiness for each individual. People may pursue happiness differently; they certainly require different elements to achieve it and surely have different rates of success in their pursuit. But by and large it is the same happiness for everyone.

In the following chapters we shall consider some of the elements and experiences of life that are and are not related to happiness—love, sex, age, money, religion, and so on. Most of the evidence deals with how particular factors are associated with happiness, whether those who have a great deal of love, good sex, high incomes, etc., are happier than those who have less of these; and how the factors themselves are interrelated, how combinations of them are related to happiness. It is important to realize that when we find that people who love and are loved are happier than others, it does not prove that this love *produced* happiness. Nor does it mean that love always makes you happy, or that love is even necessary for happiness. All it shows is that love and happiness tend to go together. In other words, in these chapters we will be talking about who is happy and who is not.

3. Happy People

Before asking who is happy and why, let us draw a more general picture. Knowing how happy most people say they are puts the rest of the information into a context. And knowing how happy people describe themselves tells us something about what they mean by happiness.

Happiness

We are generally quite happy. Each survey that asked Americans how happy or satisfied they are used somewhat different questions, different language (happiness, satisfaction, etc.), different sampling methods; they asked these questions at different times; and of course, they asked different people. Yet the results were remarkably similar. Most of the people in the country say that they are at the upper end of the happiness or satisfaction scale. Sixty percent of the people who replied to our *Psychology Today* questionnaire said that they had been "moderately happy" or "very happy" over the last six months; women responding to the *Good Housekeeping* survey reported even more happiness—70 percent had been "moderately happy" or "very happy" over the last six months. And in a careful national survey by Frank Andrews and Stephen Withey, 53 percent were "delighted" or "pleased" at their level of happiness, while a full 86 percent were "mostly satisfied" or better.

A small but substantial group feels quite unhappy and dissatisfied. The percentage unhappy is even more consistent than the percentage happy; 9 percent to 13 percent say that they are moderately or very unhappy. This is not a large percentage, but we should not necessarily take these figures to mean that most of us are in good shape. People tend to answer questions of this sort in a positive way. If you ask someone you just met, "How are you?" he usually replies, "Fine." He might just have had a serious car accident, lost a loved one, broken up a marriage, or been fired from a job; but he will still say "Fine," or, at worst, "Not bad." This is a familiar result of research in psychology. Therefore the actual numbers are less important than the fact that we do have people at both ends—delighted and miserable—and that most are toward the positive end. When we see in later chapters that some people are happier than others, we should consider this in the context of a population that, by and large, says that it is satisfied and happy. In other words, we shall be describing and explaining variations among people who claim to be fairly well off.

Optimism

Although the United States has been going through difficult times—high unemployment and inflation, a loss of faith in government, and a general disenchantment with traditional values—people remain wonderfully optimistic about their own lives. Almost 70 percent of the people say they are very optimistic or moderately optimistic about life in general, and only 6 percent say that they are pessimistic. In other words, only about one person in seventeen has a dim view of the future—the rest are either neutral or positive. In addition, people expect their own lives to improve. In every survey that has been done, no matter when, between 60 and 70 percent of the people predict that they will be happier or more satisfied in ten years than they are now; and only about 4 percent say they will be less happy. This result is remarkable: remember that it comes from people who *already* describe themselves as quite happy, who nevertheless expect to become happier still.

Curiously, this optimism does not carry over to feelings about the country. Only 30 percent are very or moderately optimistic about the future of the United States, while almost as many, over 20 percent, are pessimistic. Overall, the people are split just about in half between optimistic and pessimistic visions of the country's future. It is surprising that people retain their optimism about their own lives despite their more negative view of their society, but this result is consistent with the next point.

The Grass Is Not Greener

People think they are happier than other people. When asked to compare their happiness or satisfaction with that of the average person in the country, 62 percent said they were better off than the average, 25 percent said they were the same as the average, and only 13 percent described themselves as less well off than others. This is a fascinating finding because it is often thought that comparisons play a crucial role in producing happiness. We are said to look at other people's lives and imagine that their marriages are happier, their sex lives sexier, their incomes higher, their grass in fact green and the comparison supposedly makes us dissatisfied. It turns out that most people think they are better off than others (except, as we shall see, when it comes to sex) and also consider themselves happy. Whether these two are causally related is unclear, but it does seem apparent that comparing ourselves with others is not a major source of unhappiness.

Good and Bad Times

Even for those who say they are very happy, life is a mixture of good and bad. In one survey, people were asked which of various emotions or feelings they had experienced over the last few weeks. Sixty percent had at least once felt "excited," "pleased," "proud," and that "things are going my way"; and a full 30 percent had felt "on top of the world" at least once. This response, I think, indicates that these people really did feel good about life; they were not, as I suggested earlier, just using the top of the scale because that is customary. To feel "on top of the world" is a fairly distinct sensation that most of us understand, though not all of us have felt it often. When almost a third of the people experience it in a two- or three-week period, they are enjoying life.

On the other side of the coin, these same people report feeling negative emotions with some regularity, though not as often as the positive emotions. Fifty percent felt "restless" once or more, a quarter felt "lonely" or "bored," and almost a third felt "depressed" at least once, with a fifth feeling depressed several times or more over a few-week period. This implies that many people, more than might be suggested by their answers to the overall happiness question, are having bad times. To feel depressed several times in a few weeks is, probably, to feel very unhappy during that period. Americans may say that they are happy—and indeed many of them do experience considerable happiness—but their happiness does not defend them from depression and loneliness. There is no question that life is extremely satisfying for most Americans, especially when compared to citizens of other nations, but it is far from perfect.

The Elements of Happiness

In our surveys, we asked people to rate their happiness with life in general and also with more specific elements of life—love, income, friends, personal growth, sex, and so on. From the high overall level of happiness, one would expect that the various parts of their lives would also be rated high. That is true. But there is considerably variation—people are much more satisfied with some aspects of life than with others. In the chapters that follow we shall examine the most important of these elements in detail. But they can also be grouped into three areas.

The social elements—marriage, family, friends, children—are all rated very high. Almost everyone says he is satisfied with these parts of his life. As we shall see, this conflicts directly with a great deal of evidence that marriage in particular is a great source of conflict in our society, and that many people are uncertain about having children. Nevertheless, as a superficial description, people say they are happy with these areas of life. They also say that the social elements of life are the strongest influence on whether or not they are happy.

Economic elements—job, income, standard of living—are rated considerably lower. Although most people are happy with these areas, they are less happy than with life's social aspects. However, our other findings show that these concerns have much less effect on happiness in general than social concerns, that this lack of satisfaction with economic considerations matters less than we might have thought.

Personal elements—success, developing oneself, accomplishing something in life, freedom and independence—are also rated low in terms of how happy people are with them. Again, most people are reasonably satisfied, but considerable dissatisfaction exists. And the most common complaint was that people did not have time to do the things they wanted to do. Perhaps the pace of life or the competition to get ahead was interfering with the other things people preferred doing.

The Pillars of Happiness—A Brief Preview

In considering these elements of life, we shall see that some are much more closely related to general happiness than others. People can be very happy with certain aspects of life—for example, where they live and their religious feelings and experiences—and still be extremely unhappy. These elements seem to play a relatively small role in happiness for most people. In contrast, those who are happy with other aspects of their lives—for example, love and marriage—are very likely to be happy in general.

In two studies we asked people how happy they

THE TEN PILLARS OF HAPPINESS

RANK	SINGLE MEN	SINGLE WOMEN	MARRIED MEN	MARRIED WOMEN
1.	Friends and social life	Friends and social life	Personal growth	Being in love
2.	Job or primary activity	Being in love	Being in love	Marriage
3.	Being in love	Job or primary activity	Marriage	Partner's happiness
4.	Recognition, success	Recognition, success	Job or primary activity	Sex life
5.	Sex life	Personal growth	Partner's happiness	Recognition, success
6.	Personal growth	Sex life	Sex life	Personal growth
7.	Finances	Health	Recognition, success	Job or primary activity
8.	House or apartment	Body and attractiveness	Friends and social life	Friends and social life
9.	Body and attractiveness	Finances	Being a parent	Health
10.	Health	House or apartment	Finances	Being a parent

were with each of many aspects of their lives and also how happy they were in general. We then looked at the relationship between each of the separate aspects and overall happiness. Naturally, being happy with any part of life tends to make you happier in general, but some things count much more than others. The list on page 39 shows how the individual parts of life ranked in terms of their relationship to general happiness. Remember, this is not how important people *think* each part is, but rather how important it seems to *be* when we compare their happiness on each part with their overall happiness.

The Person Most Likely

Who is most likely to be happy? After analysis of all the results of our studies and many others, we can say that the happiest person on the North American continent is a forty-year-old Unitarian clergywoman. She lives in Canada and works full-time. She is married for the first time, is in love with her husband and is loved equally by him, has an active, satisfying sex life. She has a college degree (no graduate education), earns twenty-five thousand a year. Both she and her husband are in good health. She is not especially religious, does not believe in ESP, has had peak experiences, has at times felt in harmony with the universe, has confidence in herself and in her guiding values; she believes that life has meaning and direction and that she has control over both the good and bad things that happen to her. She is not fat.

We can also say that this description is ridiculous. It simply combines those elements that we know are related to happiness, and this kind of combination rarely makes any sense. In fact, if we have learned anything from our study of happiness, it is that there are no simple answers. The people who tell us that they are very happy are so different from one another in so many ways that the notion of a "recipe for happiness" is obviously inappropriate. Here are just a few examples:

Happy: A thirty-three-year-old man with no children and not planning to have any. He and his wife are both teachers and together earn about twenty-five thousand dollars a year. He considers himself bisexual and has had sexual relations with more than forty people but is very dissatisfied with his sex life. He is in love with his wife but thinks he loves her more than she does him. He lacks confidence in his guiding values, but is sure his life has meaning and direction and feels that he has control over the things that happen to him. This man is quite religious, believes in a personal God and in the afterlife. He grew up and lives in a small town; his parents were loving toward each other and toward him. He is very happy with almost all aspects of his life—finances, job, friends, recognition, personal growth, and love. The main exceptions are his marriage and his sexual life, both of which leave him dissatisfied. Overall, he describes himself as very happy.

Happy: A forty-eight-year-old married woman with two children who works as a secretary. She earns eight thousand dollars a year and her husband, who works for the phone company, earns thirteen thousand dollars. She has had sexual intercourse with only her husband, is very satisfied with her sex life, is in love with her husband, who is the only man she has ever loved (though she thinks he loves her a little more than she loves him). She is not very religious, but does believe in God and in an afterlife, is confident of her guiding values, thinks her life has meaning and direction and that she has considerable control over what happens to her. She grew up and lives in New York; her parents were cold toward each other and to her and were divorced when she was only three years old. She does not smoke, drinks very little, and takes no drugs except vitamins. She is very or moderately happy with all aspects of her life and is optimistic about her future. She says: "I can't say that life is perfect, I don't think anything in this world is ever perfect, but my life is very, very good. I love my husband and he loves me; he is a wonderful man who makes me very happy in millions of ways. My children are a constant joy. I like my job—don't love it, but it is easy, I'm good at it, the people are nice, and it means a lot to me. Life seems very full now and has for many years. We don't do many things that other people might think exciting, but we are very happy."

Happy: A twenty-four-year-old married woman with no children who works as a salesclerk earning only six thousand dollars while her husband is a student. She has led an active sex life but is now faithful to her husband and is very satisfied. She is in love and her love is returned equally. She is not religious, but has confidence in her guiding values and thinks her life has meaning and direction, though just where it is going is unclear at the moment. She grew up in a stable, loving family, has three sisters, lives in a suburb of a large city and likes it there. She is happy with the social aspects of her life, but quite unhappy with her job, financial situation, sense of personal growth and recognition. She is also dissatisfied with herself physically because she is too tall (5 feet 10) and not attractive enough. She is very happy.

"I guess the main thing that matters right now is my husband and our life together. I hate my job—I'm only doing it so we can manage financially and would change if I ever got a chance. I want to do something that is more fun and where I can feel I'm using whatever talents I have. I want to have children but we can't afford them yet. When Fred gets through school and is making some money, we'll have kids and I won't work for a while. Right now that is in the future, but I think it will all work out. And for now, despite everything, I am really very happy. . . ."

Happy: A twenty-nine-year-old single man who has an excellent job which pays over twenty-five thousand dollars a year. He is not in love now, but has a very active social and sex life—"different girls every week." He is not religious, not sure of guiding values, not certain his life has meaning, but optimistic about the future. His parents were divorced when he was a teen-ager, but before that his father was very warm to him, his mother cool. He lives in a fairly large city (which he dislikes because he would rather be in a metropolis where there is more going on). He has taken various drugs (LSD, marijuana, cocaine, downers) but except for marijuana does not use them now. He smokes three packs of cigarettes a day and drinks quite a bit. His major complaints center around the lack of love in his life. Overall, he is very happy.

"I have a good time going out a lot, being with different girls all the time, hitting bars and nightclubs, going to parties. I also like my job and am good at it. Life is a ball. I know eventually I'll want to find someone to love and settle down—I don't see my present way of life going on for too much longer. But now it's terrific."

Happy: A seventy-nine-year-old woman who has never been married, had no sex life, few friends, and is not in good health. She is a retired physician. She believes in God, an afterlife, her own guiding values, and the meaning of life. On the other hand, she feels she has only some control over the good and bad things that happen to her. She grew up and spent most of her life in a large city, but now lives in a smaller city and wishes that she could be in a rural area. She describes herself as very happy in most aspects of her life.

"What makes me happy? The weather—the morning sun shining into my window or a soft rain falling, dripping from leaf to leaf in the vines, or a wild wind blowing the trees about. Good food: the taste of coffee or roast chicken or a genuine Chinese dinner, preferably Szechuan [a woman after my own heart]. Creativity—making things, painting a map of Middle Earth or paper sculpture, when my eyesight was better than it is now. Reading—always reading, ever since I was seven years old. If I am deprived of reading, there is no satisfactory substitute.

"But perhaps the essential thing for my happiness all my life has been freedom. Freedom to be alone or with others if I choose. Freedom to move about and choose my profession. Freedom from pressures—though one needs the stimulus of ambition and challenges.

Freedom even now, when I am physically handicapped, to use my time as I please.

"I have had much joy in travel. Human relationships mean a great deal to me. My relationships have been few but very deep. . . . While I should have liked to have been married, when I compare my life now with that of most women who had spouses and children, I think I am happier than most at this age."

Hers has not been a life most people would choose—solitary, without romance, love, and sex, most of the joys being found by and through herself. Yet she is happier than most.

Unhappy: A twenty-six-year-old married woman with no children. She works as a medical technician earning fourteen thousand dollars a year while her husband, a carpenter, earns about the same. She is in love but her partner loves her more. She has had sexual relations with sixteen different men but is now faithful to her husband. She is dissastified with her sex life. She does not believe in God but does believe in an afterlife and in ESP. She is quite confident of her guiding values, is not sure life has meaning and direction, and thinks she has only some control over what happens to her. She grew up and lives in a rural community. Her parents stayed together but were cold to each other and to her. She is moderately happy with the recognition she receives, but unhappy with most other aspects of life, including love, marriage, sex, friends, and job. Overall, she is very unhappy.

"Most of the time I feel lousy. I worry a lot about nothing, feel guilty when I haven't done anything wrong, and have all kinds of strange fears. Some days I just start crying and can't stop for a while. I think I look awful because I'm so fat (5 feet 2, 142 pounds), no one seems to like me and I don't like myself much either. I make a mess of myself with taking pills [She has tried and used regularly tranquilizers, sleeping pills, cocaine, marijuana, and LSD.] and they don't help at all. I love my husband and he loves me, but it doesn't make the world make sense or make me seem to be worth anything."

Unhappy: A forty-four-year-old divorced man who works on an assembly line at a factory, earning seventeen thousand dollars a year. From his marriage he has two children whom he sees every other weekend and occasionally in between (they are fourteen and eleven). He is quite religious, believes in God and an afterlife, and attends church regularly. He has moderate confidence in his guiding values, is sure life has meaning (though not sure what it is), but thinks he has little control over what happens to him. He has a lot of friends from work, leads an active sex life with many different women, and is in good health. He comes from a warm family, his parents were not divorced, but he was not close to his father. He is not in love and definitely misses having one person to care about. But he loves and enjoys his children. Although he is moderately happy with many parts of his life—finances, job, sex, children, recognition—overall, he is very unhappy.

"I guess some people would envy me even though I'm divorced. I have a good paying job, nice guys to work with, terrific children who I see pretty often, and I'm healthy. I go out with women as often as I want and they seem to like me so that part is OK. And at night whenever I want I stop off for a beer with people from work. But most of the time I am not satisfied. I don't have any good friends, guys I can talk to and do things with; there isn't any girl I care about; so a lot of time I feel lonely. I sit at home, watch the TV, and that's it. It isn't much, and I wonder if that's all that's left in my life. I like seeing my kids, but that's not so often and not much else gives me much happiness, if that's what you want to call it. So I work hard all week, have some drinks, go out once or twice, and so what. . . ."

There are endless examples of both happy and unhappy people. We find happy and unhappy people with almost any set of characteristics, and frequently they share the same characteristics. Young and old; religious and nonreligious; rich or with little money; living in small towns and huge cities; holding good jobs, poor jobs, or no jobs; having wild sex, conventional sex, or none at all; in love or not in love; married, single, or living together—all of these descriptions can apply to either happy or unhappy people. As we shall see, many of these elements do *play a role* in happiness: people with certain characteristics are more likely to be happy than people without them. But the overriding fact is that no one factor or small set of factors *determines* happiness. People find happiness in all sorts of ways, in all sorts of situations. They find it because of what they have in their lives or despite it. There are, in short, no easy answers to the question of what produces happiness. If there were, it might be less interesting and perhaps more attainable. The answers are almost as elusive as happiness itself. But as we shall see, some aspects of life clearly do matter a great deal.

4. Love and Sex

> *"Come live with me and be my love,*
> *And we will all the pleasures prove"*
> —CHRISTOPHER MARLOWE

There is no simple recipe for producing happiness, but all of the research indicates that for almost everyone one necessary ingredient is some kind of satisfying, intimate relationship. Sex is not far behind in importance, and marriage, that venerable institution that is to some extent a combination of the two, is still, despite all the changes in our attitudes, a crucial factor in many people's happiness. People who are lucky enough to be happy with love, sex, and marriage are more likely to be happy with life in general than any other people. Those who are unhappy with this aspect of their lives are the least likely to have found general happiness. So let us start here.

Love

A twenty-six-year-old unmarried woman with a good job, reasonable income, excellent education, and fine health tells us: "I'm well educated, have a robust personality, am liked, respected, and sought out by many. I'm a true friend, can handle responsibilities, and have gone through the death of a parent, broken love affairs, and other difficult events. I have friends, and have grown and become a very independent and strong person. I can cope with anything." Obviously a woman who has had some hard times, but feels pretty good about herself and is in a position that many would envy. Yet, she adds: "I would like to be loved, totally and completely by a man. All the great friends and family and satisfaction gained from a worthwhile job cannot fill a void of not being loved."

Love is mentioned more than anything else as the one element missing from people's lives that, if supplied, would bring happiness. Many people who seem to have everything else are unhappy or even miserable because they do not have love.

We heard from a successful man in his thirties who has a very active sex and social life, who said: "I would trade my life with anyone who was in a relationship where he was loved by a good woman." He goes on to say, quite specifically, that he has everything else that should make him happy but that he would give it all up for love. This may sound awfully romantic, though perhaps we all would like the person we love to feel "I'd give it all up for you . . ." Fortunately, one rarely has to give up everything for love, but there are many who say they would be willing to if the opportunity presented itself. People look to love as the key to happiness.

Asked to tell us what they *think* is important for their happiness, virtually everyone rates love very high. Many people who were happily in love made much of this fact and said that love made them happy; but the major emphasis on love came from those who missed it. In this respect, for most people, love is almost like water: when we have it, we take it for granted; when it is absent, all of a sudden, it becomes crucial. People who are poor do not always list money as crucial for their happiness (as we shall see); but people without love almost always list love.

Love and Age

Although we sometimes think that adolescence is the time when love is most important, most on people's minds (a young man's fancy and all that), it turns out that this is not accurate. A massive study of young men between the ages of sixteen and twenty-five asked how important love was. Love was important for almost everyone—but the men rated love more and more important as they got older. In the earlier years, friendship and self-fulfillment were considered more important than love in providing happiness, but by the time these men were twenty-three, love had become of the utmost importance.

From age twenty-five on, love continues to be rated as very important by both sexes. In all age groups from twenty-five to fifty-five, over 80 percent consider it very or moderately important to their happiness; and even among those over sixty-five, 75 percent still rate it that high, a barely noticeable drop in importance. Thus, love is important not only for innocent youngsters, romantic teen-agers, and young men and women going through their initial long-term romantic relationships or lack of them; love is important to people of all ages, including the very old.

You might think that love only matters when the "basic" necessities of life are present. We sometimes think of love as a luxury that only people who are reasonably well off can afford; that if you were very poor, unemployed, unhealthy, or were missing some other essential, you would worry less about love. This may be so for someone who is in desperate need; but we have little detailed information on those in the world who live on virtually no money, have to worry about their next meal, live without decent shelter, and so on.

However, leaving aside these extremely unfortunate people (I'll discuss them in Chapter 9), we found no relationship at all between how important people consider love and their income level, health, education, employment situation, or anything else. The poorest people who replied to our surveys had annual incomes under five thousand dollars, which is quite low by American standards. (Some of them were students, who are not comparable to families earning that little; but many were simply people with no jobs, or low-paying jobs, or older, retired people.) These very low income people rated love just as important as anyone else. They also rate money more important than richer people, but their desire for more money has no effect on how they rate other things in life. Love is rated high by rich and poor alike.

Love and Happiness

People *think* love is important for happiness, and they are right. From all of the evidence available, people who are happily in love actually are happier; being in love plays a crucial role in general happiness for both sexes, for young and old, educated and uneducated, heterosexual and homosexual—for just about everyone. People who say they are happy in terms of love are very likely to be happy in general; and love contributes at least as much to their happiness as any other factor.

In one study, satisfaction with love was much more closely related to general happiness than were satisfaction with money, health, being a parent, place of residence, and one's body; and substantially more important even than factors such as job, personal growth, recognition and success, friends, social life, and sex. With the possible exception of marriage and family, which we'll come to in the next chapter, love had the highest relationship with general happiness. The relationship is very strong; of those people in one study who said that they were very happy with the love in their lives, over 90 percent were also very happy with their lives in general and less than 1 percent were very unhappy in general.

As we discuss the influence of love, money, health, education, and other factors, we shall find that none of them provides a sure ticket to happiness. Even love, the strongest influence, leaves room for variation. We found 1 percent who were very happily in love and still unhappy, and another 3 percent who were moderately unhappy despite their great satisfaction with their love lives. Moreover, about 1 percent of the people who were very happy in general were very unhappy with their love lives. So, it is possible to have love and not be happy, and also to be happy without love. But both are very rare.

Unrequited Love

Unrequited love is probably the subject matter of more sonnets, songs, and novels than everything else put together. As this vast literature suggests, loving someone who does not return your love is a source of great unhappiness. As one woman put it, she wished the man she loved could be in her shoes so that "he would see how much I really love him and he'd know how hurt I feel, how hurt he makes me."

The pains of unreturned love are so much a part of our culture that we sometimes may assume that the opposite situation is not painful or is even ideal. So much popular fiction deals with the difficulty of finding someone to be loved by that the difficulty of finding someone to love is often given short shrift. Yet the evidence from our research indicates that loving less is almost as bad as loving more. People who loved their partner more than they were loved rated themselves only a little less happy than those in the reverse situation, while both were way below those who loved equally. The only kind of love relationship that seems to be related strongly to happiness is reciprocal love.

Love is about equally important to men and women.

They both rank it at or near the top of the list, and for both, unhappiness in love is related to general unhappiness. On the critical question of whether they love equally, the two sexes respond identically—half of each sex in a love relationship say that it is equal. However, when it is not equal, women are more likely than men to think they love more (26 percent of the women and only 18 percent of the men think their love is not returned).

This difference between the sexes concerning the role love plays in their lives and their difficulties with it may change as women feel able to pursue love more actively (asking men out on dates, etc.) but right now in our society women seem to value love somewhat more than men, to suffer its absence more, and to be made more unhappy by unsatisfactory love relationships. This is true especially because women feel more loving than loved. There is considerable question whether women are justified in this feeling. Men in our society have been taught generally to be more reticent about their emotions than women, and may be awkward in expressing care and love. They may love as much, but say less—but whether or not this is true, it is correct that women feel less loved, and as far as their happiness is concerned, their feeling is what matters. It may be that if men learn to express their tender emotions more (as some now seem to be doing), the result will be a significant increase in the happiness of women.

Love and Other Aspects of Life

Being happily in love seems to be connected closely with a wide range of things in life. People who are not happily in love have the following characteristics: they are more likely to feel worthless, to feel "I can't go on," to suffer from anxiety, to have trouble concentrating, and to feel "like a phony." The connection between a lack of love and these other negative feelings about oneself is not necessarily strong—a lack of love does not guarantee that the person will feel this way;

but there is a consistent pattern. Clearly, the individual who is not happy in love feels less good about himself or herself and, as one might expect, also considers or even tries suicide more often. This unhappiness with love is connected with more general attitudes toward life also. People who rate their love happiness low tend to believe that they cannot control the good things that happen in life and that when something is going well it probably won't last. In addition, they are less likely to think that their lives have direction and meaning or to have faith in their own guiding values. And, of course, they are lonelier and much less satisfied with their sex lives.

Lovelessness conjures up a picture of someone who thinks very little of himself, is nervous, has no faith in the world or in any particular values, and generally must face the day with gloom and sadness rather than joy and anticipation. A lack of happiness with love may not cause all of this—it is even possible that it works the other way around, that someone with all these qualities is less likely to be loved—but the pattern is clear. Lots of money, a good job, health, beauty, marriage, even sex do not make up for a lack of love.

Sex

This is the age of sex. We are freer about it than ever before, and the sex industry is big, big business. There has always been prostitution, but now we have sex films, sex books, massage parlors where middle-class men go for a little fun in the afternoon or during lunch breaks. We have dozens of magazines devoted either entirely or largely to sex—and sex of all kinds, hetero, homo, sadism, bondage, couples, swinging, switching, anything you can imagine. And we have "serious" books giving the most detailed information on sexual practices, how to do anything, when to do it, and even how often you should aim for. Sex used to be sold mostly to men, but now it is perhaps even more central to the women's movement—women are told to accept their own bodies, to expect to be multiorgasmic, to masturbate early and often, and so on. Sex has definitely come out of the closet and is being celebrated as, if not the answer to everything, certainly one of the major parts of life. A good sex life is being equated with a good life, self-acceptance, success, and in some sense the true test of a person. It should therefore come as no surprise to anyone that sex is important to happiness—if you are happy with your sex life, you are more likely to be happy with life in general. As we shall see, however, there are definite limits to the amount of happiness sex can provide.

Sex and Love

When we ask people what they think is important to their happiness, almost nine out of ten say that sex is "moderately" or "very" important. But the number ranking it at the top ("very important") is much lower (44 percent) than those who consider love at the top of the list (57 percent). Similarly, very few people mention sex as one of the crucial things missing from their lives. They do not seem to think that sex alone will make much of a difference to their happiness in the long run.

It is interesting that very few people mention sex as the major reason why they would like to change lives with someone, though one person did write that "I would change lives with anyone who had a decent sex life." The main exception to this occurs when someone wants to change lives with a particular person for a combination of love and sex—that is, they are in love with and desire someone who is in love with someone else, so our lovelorn soul wants to change lives with that loved one. One man of twenty-six wrote exactly this: "I wish I were my best friend, Frank, because he is married to the girl I love. I don't envy him in any other way, but having her to hold and make love to would make me happy." I think it is fair to say that lack of sex is not the real reason for changing in this and similar cases—it is love.

On the other hand, people do occasionally want to be someone partly because of their assumed sexual activities. Hugh Hefner is picked for his bunnies; Mick Jagger is chosen for his apparently unbounded sex appeal; Roger Vadim is selected because he has been with a long list of beautiful women (Bardot, Fonda, etc.). In these cases, sex is definitely a large part of the appeal, but since in each instance other things are mentioned—Hefner's money and fame, Jagger's talent and jet-set life; Vadim's films and style—it is just as definitely only part of it. I was fascinated by the fact that, as you may have noticed, only men are chosen because of their sexual lives. No woman wanted to be some other woman because of the sex life she led. No one, of either sex, wanted to change lives with Jane Fonda because she had been with Roger Vadim, Donald Sutherland, and presumably lots of other attractive men; not one woman wanted to be Joanne Woodward solely in order to sleep with Paul Newman; no woman mentioned the availability of sex as a reason for switching lives with someone. Many women complained about their own sex lives; many said that they wanted to be more attractive and to be found more attractive by more exciting men; many wanted to trade their lovers (or lack of them) for Robert Redford or some other notable man. But this was never the focus of their attention when they thought about whose life they would like to lead.

Many people are unhappy with their sex lives and many think this is an important lack, but almost no one seems to think that sex alone will bring happiness. Romance and love were often listed as crucial missing ingredients, but not sex; it was simply not mentioned.

Yet sex is clearly an important element in general happiness. People who are satisfied and happy with sex tend to be happy with the rest of their lives. The relationship is quite strong, though not quite as strong as between love and happiness. If you are happy with your sex life you are more likely to be happy in general than if you are not happy with sex; and similarly, if you are not happy with sex, you are less likely to be happy in general. The realtionship is far from perfect—you can be happy without a good sex life, and you can have a good sex life and be unhappy.

Quality and Quantity

The number of sexual partners people have had varies greatly. Our surveys provided a series of choices ranging up to "more than 40". Six percent of those who answered were virgins and 36 percent had been with only one person. At the opposite extreme, 5 percent had had more than forty sexual partners, and some of them wrote in actual numbers that went much higher (some of the figures were quite spectacular, though they agreed well with those obtained in other surveys specifically designed to study sexual behavior).

Yet the number of sexual partners mattered very little in terms of happiness or even satisfaction with sex. As long as there was some sexual activity, there was essentially no relationship between how many people a person had had sex with and how happy he or she was in general or about sex. The swinging attitude popularized by *Playboy* notwithstanding, most people do not find that more is necessarily better, at least if more is defined as numbers of partners.

A bit more surprising is the fact that even frequency of sex is not terribly important, as far as we can tell. Here our range was from never—no sexual intercourse during the past six months—to more than once a day (and again, some people wrote in higher frequencies than that). Perhaps we made a mistake in asking the question in terms of sexual intercourse. We meant to include a range of sexual relations—traditional male-female intercourse, oral and anal sex, homosexual relations, and so on. We know that some people understood it this way, but probably some did not. However, self-masturbation was clearly excluded even though this is a common form of sexual expression. Thus, our question dealt with sexual activity between people, not what one person can do for himself or herself.

Although it would be nice to have more information about celibacy and masturbation in relation to general happiness, the questions we chose probably got most of what is important. Recent publications that idealize masturbation as the perfect sexual outlet (especially for women) may do a world of good for those who consider it unnatural or just never consider it at all. Masturbation clearly does provide physical satisfaction and for some people can play a substantial role in their sexual lives. But it seems highly unlikely that it can fully replace sex with another person. All of the evidence from this and other studies is that sexual satisfaction is closely related to having sex with someone else.

To return to the original point: frequency of sex is, in a sense, twice removed from happiness. That is, frequency is somewhat related to sexual satisfaction (the more often you have sex, the more likely you are to be satisfied with your sex life), and sexual satisfaction is related to general happiness. But the correlation between frequency and happiness is very slight. A closer look at the data explains why; it turns out that the correlation between frequency and satisfaction can be accounted for almost entirely by the people who have no sex life at all. *They* all tend to be extremely dissatisfied. If one removes sexually inactive people from the respondents, one discovers that frequency has only a minuscule relationship even to sexual satisfaction. Having sex with a lot of partners or having it every day may be good exercise and a lot of fun for some people, but it is not the critical element in either sexual satisfaction or happiness. Good sex—whatever that is—counts for a lot; quantity counts little.

By contrast, though frequency and number of partners play small roles, love plays a big role in sexual satisfaction. People who are in love and feel their love is not returned tend to be less happy with their sex lives than those in an equal love relationship. This, of course, is what we have always been told, but in recent years there has been some questioning of this love-sex relationship. With freer attitudes toward sex, many more people have sexual relations without being in love, and at times there seems to be a tendency for some people to treat love and sex as more or less independent issues. Our evidence, however, provides strong support for the more traditional notion that love and sex are bound together. Not that you cannot have love without sex; not that you cannot have sex without love. But love without sex and sex without love appear to be less fully satisfying than the combination of the two.

Age and Sex

It isn't just the youngsters who think sex is important or who worry about their sex lives. People of all ages say that sex is an important factor in their happiness, though the percentage ranking it very high decreases somewhat over the age of about fifty-five. There is reason to believe that even when people are much older than that, as old as seventy-five or more, sex remains important to many of them; they retain sexual capacity and are frustrated and unhappy if they do not have some sexual outlet. Naturally, as people get older, their sexual drive and ability decreases somewhat. The frequency with which people want sex and with which they are able to perform sexually declines somewhat with age. But not as much as one might think, and in general older people are still both capable and interested.

Many writers have made this point, but I think it is worth repeating. For some reason, our society, which is so open about sexuality these days, continues to think of sex in old age as dirty or obscene or perhaps ridiculous. A "dirty old man" seems to refer to any old man who is interested in sex, not just one who has perverse sexual habits. We seem to feel that something is wrong with an older person who is still interested in sex, and we do everything we can to make it difficult for older people to have sex lives. Nursing homes, for example, segregate men and women and are shocked when the two sexes get together for anything more than bridge or canasta. For fifty or sixty years it was fine for these people to engage in sexual relations—indeed, they were unhealthy, inhibited, prudish if they didn't—but suddenly, because their hair is gray, we tell them they should repress their sexual feelings. We treat our old people the way we treat young children: don't touch yourself there, don't play with each other's sex organs.

Yet every study shows that people continue to have sexual urges even when they are very old, and that their happiness depends in part on satisfying these urges. It is difficult to get accurate, reliable figures on sexual activity, but those we have indicate that sexual activity declines only gradually with age. The most active period is naturally from about twenty to thirty years of age, but there is only a slight decline up until fifty-five. After fifty-five, the decline becomes noticeable but is still quite gradual. For example, among a group of women over fifty-five, discounting those who were widowed and not remarried, the average frequency of sex was about every other week—twice a month. While this may not sound terribly high, it should be compared to the average of younger women, which is only slightly more than once a week.

Perhaps more important, older women report considerable satisfaction with their sex lives. In one survey, 52 percent said they were very or somewhat satisfied, which is not that much less than the 60-65 percent we find among younger women in the same survey. The frequency of sex has decreased as women get older, but apparently it is about what they want.

However, we should not forget those widowed and divorced women. Of course, the number of women in this situation becomes larger as the sample group becomes older, and being alone tends to have disastrous effects on one's sex life. Divorced and widowed women who have not remarried and are not living with someone are quite dissatisfied with their sex lives—only 20 percent of the widowed womn and 40 percent of the divorced women are even somewhat satisfied. We shall return to a discussion of the effects of marriage and divorce in a moment. For now, the important point is that either state reduces sexual satisfaction and that in turn has a negative effect on general happiness.

Specific Sexual Problems

Many people told us that they suffered from specific sexual problems. A fifth of the men had premature ejaculations, and substantial numbers had trouble with impotence, inability to become aroused, and trouble reaching orgasm. But many more women had difficulties. Indeed, this is one of the most dramatic contrasts between the sexes. A fifth of the women suffered from inability to become aroused, 10 percent from painful intercourse, and 8 percent from postcoital depression. All of these figures, while troubling, are approximately comparable to similar difficulties for men. The shocker is the category labeled "trouble reaching orgasm." Fewer than 10 percent of the men list this as a problem whereas 38 percent of the women do—more than a third of all the women who responded to our survey had trouble reaching orgasm.

To make matters worse, these sexual problems are more closely related to happiness for women than for men. For some reason, men who suffered from any of the difficulties just mentioned were in general just as happy as men who didn't. These men had some sexual troubles, but apparently they made little difference in their lives. In contrast, women who had sexual problems were less happy than women who did not. The major reason for this difference may be that most men eventually do achieve orgasm. Impotence, the one difficulty that might have disastrous effects on their sex lives and perhaps on their lives in general, troubles only 5 percent of men and even these may experience difficulty only occasionally. It has been suggested that the women's movement has produced more sexually aggressive women who know what they want, want to be satisfied, and are more likely to blame the man if they are not. Further, it has been argued that this puts pressure on men to "perform" and that this pressure is causing male sexual problems, especially impotence.

All of this may be true, but we found only 5 percent of men who suffered from impotence among a population of highly educated men who might be expected to be just the ones involved with "liberated women." And these men did not suffer enough for impotence to have any noticeable effect on their overall happiness.

But women who have sexual problems are less happy and probably it is because they do not achieve orgasm. Those 38 percent who have trouble reaching orgasm often do not reach it at all, or have so much trouble that it makes the whole experience unsatisfying or even unpleasant. Although I said earlier that masturbation was not by itself an ideal sexual outlet and would not by itself lead to full sexual satisfaction for most people, surely masturbation would be a big help to those who cannot achieve orgasm through sexual intercourse or through other sexual relations with someone else. Masters and Johnson have suggested that sexual satisfaction through masturbation can be a first step toward achieving satisfaction in other forms of sexual activity.

One surprising and paradoxical finding regarding sex emerged from our surveys. Although women are much more likely than men to suffer from a serious sexual problem, the men report being more dissatisfied with sex in general. Over fifty percent of the men in one sample said they were moderately or very dissatisfied with their sex lives, while only 30 percent of the women were dissatisfied. Given their admitted sexual problems, this is difficult to understand. One possibility is that even today women ask and expect less from sex than men. (On average, women do think sex is slightly less important to their general happiness than men do.) Another possibility is that, in fact, women are having better sex lives than men in some absolute sense. I doubt it: for one thing, 38 percent of the women have difficulty achieving orgasm while only 33 percent say they are even moderately dissatisfied with sex. One would think that the full 38 percent would be dissatisfied, along with some of the orgasmic women. It is more likely that women say they are satisfied because they expect little.

We have seen that women suffer from specific sexual problems more than men and that these problems, when experienced by women, are related to general happiness. We have also seen that women are more often the victims of unrequited love, or think they are. Taken together these two findings suggest that women are having more difficulty with their romantic-sexual relationships than men are. Given these facts, it is surprising and perhaps heartening that, on average, women say they are just as happy as men. The sexes seem to have somewhat different problems, but also have different sources of satisfaction. However, a more pessimistic view is that women only say they are happy. The possibility that they are deceiving themselves will be discussed in the next two chapters, which deal with marriage and then with the differences between men and women in marriage.

Comparison with Others

One popular theory of happiness is that it depends at least in part on comparing ourselves to other people. If you make ten thousand dollars and everyone else makes more, you feel bad; if everyone else makes less, you feel good.

We shall discuss income later, in Chapter 9, but this theory is quite interesting when it is applied to sex. When something is more or less hidden from public view, like sex, we have lots of room for fantasy. It is fairly easy to look next door, notice the new TV and car and extension on the house, and know that the Smiths are raking it in, but it's difficult to observe much about the Smiths' sex life. Fantasy goes to work.

When it does, people tend to assume that their neighbors are having more sex with more people and are more satisfied with it than they themselves. Almost everyone overestimates the number of sexual partners their peers have had. (They particularly underestimate the number of virgins in the population.) A fifth of all people say they are very dissatisfied with their own sex lives, but only 3 percent think their peers are as unhappy.

If comparisons with others affect a person's happiness, then this tendency to imagine that everyone else is having sex with dozens of people, three times a day and in unimaginable positions, ought to be a source of unhappiness. If other women are having multiple orgasms in vast numbers and of indescribable intensity, your own single orgasm, no matter how pleasurable, may seem paltry. If everyone else is using ten different positions and four varieties of vibrator, your own preference for a few positions without electric aids may seem boring. Yet there is no evidence to support this idea that comparisons affect people's happiness with their sex lives. Yes, most people think that others are more active sexually than themselves, have more sex partners, and have sex more often. But we do not find a relationship between a person's own sexual satisfaction and his or her view of other people's sexual behavior or satisfaction. To put it another way, what you think others are doing sexually seems to have little effect on how satisfied you are with your own sex life or your life in general.

On average, those who think that others have many more sexual partners than they do themselves are nevertheless not especially dissatisfied with their own sex lives unless they are totally inexperienced sexually. Similarly, those who imagine others have sex more frequently than they do are just as happy with their sex lives as those who think they are more active sexually than other people. Again, the only effect is on those who have virtually no sexual activity. In other words, people who lead a reasonably active sex life do not seem to be affected much by their estimates of what others are doing. They may at times envy the wild sex lives supposedly led by other people, they may fantasize about having the same kind of lives themselves. Although few people have tried swinging sex (partner swapping and group sex), many more have thought about it. Yet if this envy or fascination with others' sex

ves does exist, it has no appreciable effect on people's
itisfaction with their own sex lives. In this area of life,
mparisons do not seem to be especially important. It
 what you do and how satisfying you find it that
atters.

Sexual Preference

y liberation has appeared to open up possibilities for
ual preference that were barely imagined not so
iy years ago. Not only have homosexuals pro-
ned and affirmed their sexual preferences in pub-
but the whole idea of "different" sexual choices has
e out of the closet. Sexually oriented magazines
 as *Playboy* and *Penthouse* have, of course, pub-
l many articles on diverse sexual preferences for
time; but recently more traditional, "family"
zines have fastened on this as a topic of consider-
eneral interest. There are now magazines devoted
ly to nonheterosexual sexuality of all kinds—ho-
uality for all, for men, for women; bisexuality;
asochism; swinging; and so on. Everything seems
e, and anything that is possible seems to be
3ut how does this new freedom to choose affect
ess? Specifically, how does it affect the hap-
of people whose sexual preferences are not
conventionally heterosexual?
nteresting to note that the number of homosex-
the population has changed very little despite
t   latic change in attitudes and freedom. In 1948,
a   f a century ago, Kinsey reported that about 4
p   f the population was exclusively or mainly ho-
m   . Today those figures have barely changed;
vi   every study finds just about 4 percent are
m   omosexual. Since Kinsey, there has been a
sli   ease in the number of people who consider
the   bisexual—most of this increase among the
you   may not yet have decided—but it is not
tru   ast numbers of homosexuals have come out
of   et or been produced by the new permis-
sive   /e are far from understanding why some

people are heterosexual and others homosexual and still others mixed, but it seems clear that even major changes in societal attitudes have relatively little effect on this phenomenon.

We have only a small number of homosexuals and people with other variations in sexual preference in all of our surveys, so the information about them should not be considered definitive. However, based on these few hundred people, we can describe some important differences and similarities between those with strictly heterosexual preferences and the others. Our sample is broad enough that it can be divided into the exclusively heterosexual (by far the largest group), the principally heterosexual who have an occasional homosexual experience or just homosexual urges; bisexuals; the principally homosexual who have some heterosexual experiences or urges; and the exclusively homosexual. We also have both males and females, somewhat more of the former, but not enough to do careful analyses to see if there are differences between the sexes. All of the results seem to hold for both, but we would need more instances to be certain of this.

Sexual Activity among Homosexuals

It may come as a surprise to some people that the frequency of sexual relations is about the same for all groups. Exclusively heterosexual people are slightly more active in terms of the average frequency with which they have sexual relations (about once or twice a week). Those calling themselves bisexuals are somewhat less active. All the other groups are about the same. However, the differences are small and may be accounted for by many factors such as the number of people who are married or living together in each group. In any case, the stereotype of the wildly active sex life of the homosexual is not borne out by the data.

Another stereotype, that homosexuals have more sexual partners during their lifetime than heterosexuals, does seem to be true. The biggest difference among our various groups in terms of sexual activity is that the exclusively homosexual person has by far the most sexual partners. The heterosexuals who replied had had the fewest partners. Most of them had had sexual relations with between two and six people, with 75 percent of the nonvirgins having had fewer than twenty partners. The same is true of those who are mainly heterosexual or bisexual. Principally homosexual people are somewhat more active, but the difference is slight. Exclusively homosexual people are different. Almost half have had more than twenty partners, and a full third more than forty. Among the other groups an occasional person may be this active, but it is rare. Among homosexuals it is typical.

Personal Background and Sexual Preference

The information we have includes some interesting data about the personal histories of people with various sexual preferences. We asked many questions about people's childhoods. Remember, however, that these were asked and answered many years after childhood ended and the answers may be inaccurate. The answers may involve distortions, errors, and guesses. Moreover, even during childhood, children often do not have a clear picture of the relationship between their parents, and may distort the way their parents treat them. Thus, these data are at best suggestive.

One question asked about parents' attitudes toward sex—were they liberal or conservative? The answers are totally unrelated to the sexual preferences of the adults answering the questions. Whether one's parents were liberal, conservative, or middle-of-the-road appears to have little impact on one's later sexual preference. As you might expect, most people said that their parents were conservative regarding sex; but there were no substantial differences among the groups.

However, the relationships between the parents and between parents and child do relate closely to sexual preference. Almost 60 percent of those who are exclusively heterosexual or exclusively homosexual say that their parents had a warm and loving relationship with each other. This is a pattern we shall see frequently— people who have an exclusive sexual preference, whether heterosexual or homosexual, resemble each other more than they resemble those with a mixed preference. Exclusivity seems more important than preference. Thus, while 60 percent of those with an exclusive preference say that their parents' relationship was good, only about half (51 percent) of the mainly heterosexual and bisexual say so. And only a third (33 percent) of the mainly homosexual do—a dramatic difference.

A person's relationship with his or her mother shows a similar though weaker pattern. Not quite 80 percent of the exclusively homosexual say they had a warm, loving mother; almost as many (74 percent) of the exclusively heterosexual report a warm and loving relationship with their mothers; while the other groups are considerably lower (about 60 percent).

But the big difference is in relationships to the father, and here the pattern changes. To begin with, all groups report far fewer good relationships with their fathers than with their mothers. Whereas overall, close to 70 percent had good relationships with their mother, only a little more than 40 percent did with their father. Whatever the reason—it may have a lot to do with fathers in past years working and most mothers not—it is certainly a striking difference. And the effect, if there is one, seems to be on homosexuals primarily. The heterosexual groups (exclusively heterosexual and mainly heterosexual) both report similar paternal relationships—about 50 percent had good ones and 20 percent bad ones. But both homosexual groups and the bisexuals had much worse relationships with their father—only 35 percent good ones and 40 percent bad ones. Whether this bad relationship caused the sexual preference, is a distortion in memory, is an accident, or is associated with other functions is unclear; but obviously, the homosexuals and bisexuals showed a strong tendency to remember that their fathers did not treat them well. Note that this is true for both males and females.

One other factor shows a substantial relationship to sexual preference: adolescent attractiveness. There is a common belief that people become homosexuals in part because for some reason they do not do well with members of the opposite sex, especially during the critical years of adolescence. This failure, it is supposed, causes them to search for satisfaction among their own sex, or perhaps to return to (or never change from) childhood sexuality, which typically is homosexual in nature. One attribute that might be expected to affect popularity in adolescence is attractiveness, and, indeed, both homosexual groups are more likely than any of the others to describe their adolescent attractiveness as below average. Over 50 percent say they were below average compared to less than 40 percent for the other groups. Moreover, only 6 percent of the exclusively homosexual say they were above average in attractiveness, while 25 percent of the heterosexuals felt they were above average. As usual, we cannot be sure this is accurate—the homosexual people may just remember it that way, or perhaps they thought they were unattractive when actually they were terrific looking. But this is the way they see it, and that may be more important than reality.

So, to sum up, two patterns emerge from childhood. Exclusively oriented people's parents had better relationships with each other, and their mothers had better relationships with them. But homosexuals had worse relationships with their fathers and felt themselves to be less attractive during adolescence. There is, of course, a great deal of variation in all of this—some homosexuals had wonderful relationships with their fathers and were very attractive. The pattern does not apply to everyone, but it suggests some factors that might be important in the development of sexual preferences.

Sexual Preference and Attitudes
Toward Love and Sex

Although their patterns of sexual relations and child-hood relationships differ somewhat, heterosexuals and homosexuals seem quite similar in the value they place on love and sex. Those who consider themselves exclusively hetero- or homo-sexual both consider love and sex of extreme importance to their happiness. Once again, we see that people with an exclusive preference, whether homosexual or heterosexual, are more like each other than they are like people with mixed sexual orientations. Although these people, too, consider love and sex important, they rate both of them substantially lower—as compared with such factors as income, health, and so on—than do those with unmixed sexual preferences. This is especially true of those who are mainly homosexual but have some heterosexual inter-ests—they rate both love and sex lower than anyone else.

These findings regarding the exclusively homosexual are especially important considering the common view that such people consider sex very important but worry less about love than heterosexuals do. Perhaps this view is less widespread than it used to be before there was more public discussion of homosexuality; but I think some people still feel that homosexuals cannot love or appreciate love in the same way as heterosex-uals. The evidence from our surveys is that this is not true. Homosexuals are virtually identical to heterosex-uals in their attitudes toward the roles love and sex play in their lives, and in their estimates of the impor-tance of sex and love for happiness. It is the other groups, the people with mixed sexual orientations, who are different.

Preference and Happiness

This leads us to happiness itself. Here, at the heart of the matter, the similarity between those with exclusive sexual preferences and their difference from those with mixed preferences are even more pronounced. On almost every measure, every indication of satisfaction with life, and especially those aspects of life that might be thought to be related to sexuality, the exclusive homosexual and the exclusively heterosexual are almost indistinguishable. And many of our stereotypes, both good and bad, simply do not hold up.

Surely, it is "common knowledge" that homosexuals suffer more from loneliness and guilt than heterosexuals. After all, we are told, homosexuals do not form lasting relationships and they must accordingly be alone much of the time, or with people they do not care about. And guilt goes without saying. Most of the theories about the origins of homosexuality involve abnormal attitudes toward sex that cause people to turn from sex between man and woman to homosexuality. Well . . .

It is true that few heterosexuals say that they regularly experience guilt as adults, but the figures are just about the same for homosexuals. About a fifth of the population seems to feel guilt often, regardless of sexual preference. The only exception is the mainly homosexual people, those who have some heterosexual dealings as well: about a third of them feel guilt often.

As for loneliness, it is a widespread problem among homosexuals. Almost 40 percent of exclusively homosexual people report it. But exactly as high a percentage of the heterosexual population reports the same thing. It is no worse, no better, for homosexuals. It is somewhat worse for mainly heterosexual and bisexual people, almost 50 percent of each group feeling lonely. And it is worst of all for the mainly homosexual, the least happy group, with over 55 percent complaining of loneliness.

And when you ask people how happy they are with love and sex, again those with unmixed orientation fare the best, though once more, people in general are not doing terribly well. Just over 50 percent of hetero- and homo-sexuals say they are very or moderately satisfied with their sex lives—the greater number of partners of the homosexuals makes them neither more nor less satisfied than heterosexuals. But bisexuals are less satisfied (only 44 percent are very or moderately satisfied), mainly heterosexual people less satisfied still (34 percent), and the principally homosexual way down at the bottom, with only 23 percent, less than a quarter, finding substantial sexual satisfaction.

You might think that bisexuality would be the best of all worlds, at least sexually, with more partners to choose from and more varieties of sexual activity to engage in. Yet bisexuals are among the least sexually satisfied, and all the others who can have sex with both sexes are also less satisfied than people who are attracted to only one sex.

When it comes to love, the results are almost the same. The exclusively oriented of either preference do the best, with 56 percent being very or moderately happy with their love relationships; the partly hetero- and bi-sexual do worse—only 45 percent happy; and the partly homosexual do the worst with only a third, 33 percent, happy. At the opposite end, those who are very or moderately unhappy, the pattern is repeated. Once more, it is clear that many people are unhappy with love; and once more, it is better to have exclusive sexual tastes. Among homo- and hetero-sexuals 30 percent say they are unhappy; with the partly heterosexual it goes up to 37 percent; with bisexuals to 47 percent; and among the mainly homosexual a whopping 56 percent say they are unhappy with love.

It is worth recalling that those with exclusive sexual preferences who are relatively happy with love and sex are the ones whose parents had a warm, loving relationship with each other. We should be very cautious about giving too much weight to this result, but it does suggest, tentatively, that the ability to form good relationships in adulthood comes in part from having parents who themselves have such a relationship.

When we consider reciprocity in love, the same pattern emerges. The exclusive groups are much more likely to be in a relationship in which they and their partners love equally. Approximately 50 percent of each exclusive group are in a reciprocal relationship;

40 percent of the mainly heterosexual group are; a third of the bisexuals; and only 30 percent of the mainly homosexual group. Interestingly, however, in nonreciprocal relationships, heterosexuals tend to say they are loved more than they love, while homosexuals, more than any other group, report loving more than their partner. But the important point is that on every measure of satisfaction heterosexuals and homosexuals look similar, with the mixed groups being in worse shape.

Although love and sex are important to happiness, as we have said many times, no one factor determines happiness entirely. Thus, it is not surprising that the pattern of results we have just described also shows up in the relationship of sexual preference to general happiness, though not quite as strongly. Once again, the homo- and hetero-sexuals are the happiest—with the homosexuals actually rating themselves a little bit happier than the heterosexuals. Next and close by come the mainly heterosexual and the bisexual. And much less happy, quite different from the other groups, are the mainly homosexual.

From all of this it seems clear that, at least for those people in our samples, homosexuals differ little from heterosexuals in their levels of satisfaction and happiness; while those with mixed preferences are worse off, especially the partly homosexual. It is tempting to speculate that in sex as in many other things in life conflicting values or tastes are difficult to deal with. It is hard to be a little homosexual, and apparently harder still to be a little heterosexual. Those who have taken a firm, unambiguous stand on the matter can concentrate on getting as much satisfaction and happiness out of sex and love as possible. But those who have mixed preferences may have trouble reconciling them—they cannot settle into a homosexual life because they occasionally are attracted to the opposie sex; they cannot settle into a heterosexual life because sometimes same-sex people attract them. And perhaps a difficult aspect of this is that no one in the world is entirely, automatically neutral in terms of sexual attraction. A person with mixed preferences cannot assume that a new friend will not be a sexual partner just because of the person's sex (the way an exclusively oriented person can for approximately half of the people in the world). This may cause difficulties. Whatever the reason, sexual preference, as long as the preference is clear and exclusive, matters much less in terms of happiness than most of us would have imagined. No doubt homosexuals still have many problems in our society that heterosexuals do not have to face, but overall their lives seem to be just about as happy.

5. *Wedded Bliss*

"*I would trade places with a happily married mother with a house full of bubbling little ones and a wonderful husband.*"

"*I have never known what it is to have a man put his arms around me and say I love you so much, I want you for my wife.*"

—SURVEY RESPONSES

Americans have been experimenting with alternative life styles, especially alternatives to traditional marriage. They are living together without getting married, getting married later, forming part-time, contract, and open marriages, trying group marriages, and sometimes forgetting about long-term partnerships entirely and staying single. Certainly, fewer Americans see marriage as the obvious, automatic outcome of a long-term love relationship. In various surveys we found as many as 5 percent of the people were living together in romantic, sexual relationships without being married. Even this small percentage would have been unimaginable ten years ago. Love and marriage may go together like a horse and carriage, but there aren't quite as many carriages nowadays.

In addition, marriages do not last as long as they used to. Not so long ago, marriage was assumed to be for life. Divorce was rare and socially stigmatizing—someone who was divorced was looked on as a little strange, not quite proper, perhaps not even acceptable in some circles. That simply is not true today. The divorce rate is approaching 50 percent—almost half of the marriages end in divorce. This dramatic increase in the divorce rate has created a whole new group of people in our society—the divorced, the formerly married who will probably be married again but are currently "single."

If the nature of marriage and the role it plays in our society have changed considerably in recent years, if marriage is no longer *the* answer for everyone, if it is no longer idealized to the extent it used to be, nevertheless—and this is one of the most fascinating and probably most important findings of the research on happiness—married people are happier than single people. Virtually every study of marital status and happiness has found this to be so. It does not matter how often you have been married, whether an earlier marriage broke up through divorce or death, whether you married early or late. If you are married right now, the chances are that you are happier than someone who is single. The complete story is much more complicated than this, and those other marital states must be considered, but it is striking that despite the changing attitudes toward marriage and the incredibly high divorce rate, a vast majority of our population seems to find happiness in marriage and to be unhappy if they remain single too long.

Before discussing the complexities, let us be clear that we cannot prove that marriage *produces* happiness, nor that being single prevents it. This kind of cause-and-effect relationship is almost impossible to demonstrate. It may well be that happy people tend to get married and unhappy ones to remain single. Who, after all, wants to marry someone who is miserable—and put up with the other person's unhappiness? To put it less harshly, someone who is happy is more fun to be with, seems more appealing; it is easier to fall in love with and want to marry such a person than someone who is sad and unhappy all the time.

Another possibility is that the various characteristics that make for unhappiness may also make marriage unlikely. A person with a bad job and poor health and who does not get along well with people possesses a group of characteristics that are likely to interfere with his happiness; they would also make him a less attractive person to marry. Once again, the unhappy person would be the unmarried person, not because marriage affects happiness, but because the very things that make the person unhappy keep him from getting married.

It is possible, therefore, that marriage does not cause happiness, but the evidence suggests it does. On the basis of our data plus the anecdotal reports of hundreds of people, it seems reasonable to say that not being married makes happiness harder to attain, while being married makes it easier. I am not by any means suggesting that there is anything inherently wrong with remaining single, or that single people cannot achieve happiness in this way, or—as God and the divorce statistics know—that being married guarantees happiness; but every piece of evidence indicates that for most people, marriage is the easiest road to happiness. The statistics are simple and impressive. Although, as we shall see, there are many complex aspects to the relationship of marriage and happiness, many differences between men and women and between first and second marriages, the overall picture is that 68 percent of married people and only 54 percent of single people are very or moderately happy with their lives. (For the moment I am not including people who live together. They will be discussed separately.)

Marriage and Loneliness

It seems likely that one of the reasons married people are happier is that they have someone to depend on, to spend time with, to share with. Even though many marriages do not involve perfect love relationships, and may not involve much love on either side, the spouse does provide companionship and a certain kind of social security—a guaranteed Saturday night date, someone to come home to, or whatever.

In a word, marriage should go a long way toward eliminating loneliness, that constant complaint of single people. Almost half of the single people (48 percent) say that they often felt lonely during the past year; and divorced people—those who are not remarried—experience loneliness even more. Less than half as many (21 percent) married people feel lonely.

Marriage is a much more effective antidote for loneliness for men than it is for women. Single men and women are about equally lonely. Married men, whether it is their first or second marriage, report very little loneliness—only 16 percent of married men say they felt lonely, a third of the rate for single people. In contrast, among women in their first marriage, almost a third (29 percent) still say they are lonely; and in second marriages, the figure jumps well above a third (38 percent). They are better off than singles, but marriage clearly does not have the same effect on women as it does on men. Even the happiest women (those who are married the first time) still experience loneliness—perhaps because many of these women stay home while the man leaves the house to work.

Age, Sex, and Single People

The relationship between marriage and happiness depends heavily on a person's age and sex. Single people tend to be less happy than married ones; but men and women experience this difference in different ways at different times.

A confirmed male bachelor, for example, tends to

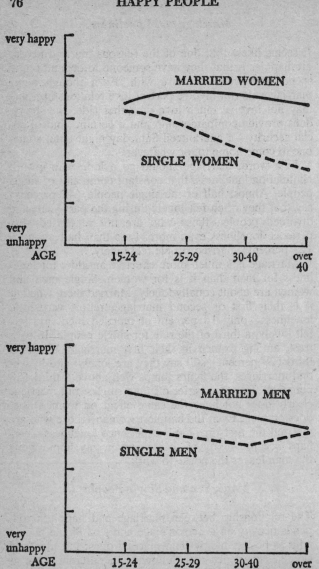

have a much easier and happier life than his female counterpart. As single men get older, they do not necessarily become less happy. On the contrary, there appears to be a point at which a single man accepts his unmarried state, settles into it, and begins to find life just fine. During their twenties and thirties, single men are less happy than married ones. But during the thirties, the difference begins to decrease somewhat: single men at this age are just about as happy as they were earlier, while married men are a little less happy than they were—still happier than their single counterparts, but the difference is smaller. Then after forty, the single men actually get happier than they were, while the married people's happiness continues to decline somewhat. By the time they are over forty, the difference between singles and marrieds has disappeared. In other words, for a man, the older he is, the easier it is to be single. As we shall see, the pattern is entirely different for women.

I have no firm explanation of this finding, but it is easy to speculate. Perhaps, as I suggested above, men get used to being single and society also gets used to their being single. Indeed, a single man becomes something of a social asset, much in demand as an "extra man" at dinner parties. If he is interested, the forty-year-old single male also has many single women available. Women frequently complain that our cultural tradition of men being older than women in romantic relationships is unfair. There is no question that such tradition exists and that it makes life a lot easier for men, especially older single men. A man who goes out with a younger woman is doing what is expected; a woman who goes out with a younger man is doing something strange. For a man of forty, women aged thirty to forty are perfectly acceptable, a woman of twenty-five might cause eyebrows to be raised but would hardly produce shock, a woman of twenty would seem "too young" but still more or less acceptable. He isn't a "dirty old man" unless he gets involved with someone under twenty. Now reverse the situation. A woman of forty can probably go out with men thirty-five and up without causing much comment. But let her be with a man in his low thirties, and she will be "fooling around" with younger men; and a man of twenty-five would be considered pretty much indecent. She will be seen as pathetic, not strong and vigorous.

Thus our forty-year-old single male has a very broad range of women among whom to choose. Assuming he has gotten used to and even prefers the single life, it can be as full of companionship as he desires—at least in theory. Getting older does not make his single life harder; in some ways it makes it easier and, as the surveys show, he finds himself happier than he was before.

Finally, and perhaps most important, society accepts older single men with no trouble at all. They are not seen as pathetic, lonely creatures; they are not dried-up spinsters (indeed there is no comparable word for men). They are "confirmed bachelors" who are often envied by married men. I am certainly not suggesting that their lives are ideal or that most men would find being single the best state for them; but society and various traditions make being single easier for men than for women, especially during middle age and after.

Age and the Single Woman

Married women of all ages seem to experience approximately the same degree of happiness. But single women get less and less happy as they get older. The difference between married and single in terms of happiness increases steadily and dramatically until single women over forty are one of our least happy groups. Looking just at single women, we see that they rate themselves quite happy during their early twenties (better than single men, though slightly less happy than married women). These single women are still fairly happy during their late twenties (about equal to single men, but by this time clearly less well off than married women). The trouble starts after the age of thirty. From this time on, single women get progressively unhappy. Why does age have this effect and why is thirty the turning point?

One obvious reason concerns childbearing. Whatever we may think about the population explosion and the need for reducing the number of babies, whatever the changes in attitudes toward having children, there is no denying the fact that most women feel strong urges to have children. This may be due to powerful biological forces or to cultural ones, but surely many women want very much to produce a child. Men also feel the urge to become parents, often just as much as or more than women. However, this parental impulse has different implications for men and women. Men can have children at virtually any age from fifteen to eighty-five. If he can still manage the sex act, no man has to say to himself, nor does his body suggest to him, that it is now or never. In contrast, the upper age for childbearing is fixed. It is unhealthy for most women to have a first child past the early thirties, and impossible much past forty. Once menopause occurs, sometime in her forties, a woman can no longer conceive a child. Every woman knows this—it is part of her biological heritage, built into her body as powerfully as her ability to have children in the first place. Thus, a woman of thirty knows that if she wants to have children it has to be pretty soon. This is all very well for married women. If their husbands want children, they can decide to have one and go about it in the time-tested way. It is an entirely different story for single women. If they want children, they have to find a man with whom to have them and in our society most women still feel that they should get married. (Of course, they can have a child without maintaining any relationship with the father or can try to adopt, but these are relatively rare and probably difficult alternatives.) Even if the single woman does not want children, she knows that a man she meets might want children and that soon she will be too old to satisfy that particular need. This biological fact of life means that for many single women time literally begins running out after the age of thirty. They realize that they must have a child soon if ever, and that time is growing short. Therein lies one source of anxiety and unhappiness for some single women over the age of thirty.

A second reason for the increasing unhappiness of single women is that their social lives become more and more difficult. The situation for older women is the reverse of that for older men. As I said earlier, a man of forty has a wide age range of women he can date; a woman of forty has a restricted range. Add to this that as people get older they are more likely to be married. Whereas the forty-year-old single man is dating younger (and therefore likely to be single) women, the forty-year-old single woman is selecting from older men, almost all of whom are already married, except perhaps the confirmed bachelors, who are dating those twenty-five-year-olds anyway. As we would expect, the data from our surveys show that single women over thirty are much less happy with their social and sex lives than either younger single women or single men at the same age. Indeed, single women over thirty are half as likely as single men of that age to be even moderately happy with their social lives. No wonder they are generally less happy as they get older.

A third reason for the unhappiness of older single women is that our society incessantly bombards us with the notion that older men are interesting and distinguished while older women are simply old. Leading men in the movies continue to be popular and to be cast in romantic roles seemingly regardlses of their age; leading women, with the exception of Katharine Hepburn and a few others, are generally in their twenties or at most their early thirties. Advertising, television, novels, and all of the mass media portray men retaining their appeal, vitality, sexuality, and strength as they get older. Not so for women, who are usually shown losing their appeal as they age. It is hardly surprising that many single women in their thirties begin to think they are losing their appeal to men, begin to doubt themselves in many ways, and are naturally unhappy.

Thus, as countless sad and ironic novels have

pointed out, single women in their late thirties and older have a rough time of it in our society. They have great trouble finding eligible males; they are often considered strange or maladjusted; they do not fit easily into social gatherings (the host or hostess who is overjoyed to find an "extra man" is burdened by an "extra woman"); and so on. I hope it is clear that I am not in any sense suggesting that this is the way it should be or must be (quite the contrary), or that this is true of all single females over the age of thirty; or even that it wouldn't be quite easy to change all of this. I am merely trying to describe the current situation, and I think it is accurate to say that a single female over thirty-five or forty has a hard time finding happiness in our society.

Parenthood

In *The Conquest of Happiness* Bertrand Russell proclaimed, "Parenthood is psychologically capable of providing the greatest and most enduring happiness that life has to offer." Many people agree. In our survey 55 percent of the people thought that being a parent was either moderately or very important to their happiness, and quite a few wrote that their greatest joy came from their children. For example, a thirty-five-year-old housewife said: "I love my husband, I have lots of friends, I enjoy my painting . . . but the one thing that matters most to me and makes me happiest is being with my children and watching them grow. When they accomplish something, I think I enjoy it even more than when I do myself." Similar comments were made by both men and women (though more of the latter) and by those who had jobs and those who did not (though again, more from the latter).

However, considering all people or just all married people, there is no discernible relationship between parenthood and general happiness. To begin, it is surprising that only 55 percent consider this an important source of happiness. This means that almost half think that having children is relatively unimportant for happiness. More to the point, happiness with one's children ranked rather low in its relationship to general happiness for both married men and married women. Married couples with children are no happier than those without. The number of children does not play any role. Even among those who are divorced, children seem to make little overall difference in happiness. Couples with children are, as you would expect, somewhat less likely to get divorced. But we have no evidence that, whether they stay together or separate, married people's happiness is related to whether or not they have children.

Having said all of this, let me add that we have relatively little information on this important question. Some surveys asked no questions about children and none explored the question deeply. My guess is that some people find great happiness in their children—perhaps as much as from any other source—but that this effect is cancelled out by equally large numbers of people whose children are directly or indirectly a source of unhappiness. Just as a child who is loving, healthy, beautiful, accomplished (you can add your own adjectives) can bring joy into its parents' lives, so a cold, unhealthy, unattractive, unaccomplished child can bring great misery. Having children can enrich a marriage or the life of a single parent, but children also bring additional burdens. Overall, parenthood ends up being neither a positive nor a negative factor in general happiness.

In this context, it is interesting to note that while attitudes toward having children appear to be changing, the percentage of people having them is not. The women's movement and concern about overpopulation have made many people question the traditional assumption that everyone should have children. Young women, and to some extent young men, no longer automatically plan to have children. They at least consider the possibility of not having any. Nevertheless, the percentage of married people who plan not to have children has not changed appreciably in twenty years. For 75 percent of the married population the answer is yes—they do want children. They want fewer children than they used to, they have them somewhat later in life, but they do have them.

Divorce

Most people who get divorced eventually remarry, but while they are divorced they describe themselves as considerably more unhappy than any other group. This varies somewhat for men and women (divorce seems to be slightly harder on women) and by age (early divorces are especially hard on women, later ones are not so bad. In one study over 20 percent of divorced women said they were very or moderately unhappy, compared to only 8 percent of married women, 15 percent of single women, and 14 percent of widows. At the other end of the scale, far fewer divorced women, compared to any other group, considered themselves very happy, half as many as married women. The figures for divorced men are only marginally less dismal. Why is divorce so difficult?

First, let us deal with the obvious reason, which is that a divorce naturally implies a bad marriage, and bad marriages are presumably always unpleasant and lead to unhappiness. When we ask someone who is divorced how happy he or she is, we are to some extent getting a reply that takes account of their miserable marriage. Even though it is over, the unhappiness it caused must cast a pall over the person for some time, so that even if their life is going well at the moment, they may tend to think of themselves as generally unhappy.

Closely related to this is that divorce usually involves some real hardships—loss of income, change of residence, taking care of children by oneself, dealing with visiting rights and so on. And adapting to a new life—suddenly being single again, dating, finding someone to go out with, loss of security, etc. In other words, the simple facts are often difficult, especially for the woman who even today is more likely to rely on her husband for financial support than vice versa, and who also almost always keeps the children, which of course is what most women want but which also places a burden on them.

I am sure I do not have to detail all of the difficulties that the shift from married to single entails. Perhaps worse than the actual hardships are the adaptation and the shock of finding that what you probably thought was permanent is now over. But other than these matters, there is the basic fact of not having a primary relationship for the moment.

Divorce and Love

It should come as no surprise that a great many divorced people suffer primarily from the lack of a romantic love relationship. They have been in one, no matter how unsatisfactory, and the divorce ends it. They are now single again, but often without some of the freedom of the single person, with greater financial burdens, perhaps children, and so on. Also, divorced people are naturally, on average, older, and this has its problems in terms of finding someone.

We found that over 60 percent of divorced people were not in a romantic relationship of any kind. As you would imagine, they were very unhappy with their sex lives (which were usually quite inactive) and their love lives. On both these counts, divorced people are much less happy than married people, and considerably less happy than single people. Clearly, this aspect of life—love, sex, romance—is the most difficult for divorced people and seems to contribute most to their unhappiness.

The special hardships visited upon women by divorce may be in part a product social traditions, such as the fact that women are discouraged from taking the initiative in asking men out on dates. One otherwise happy divorced woman pinpointed this as the source of her discontent. ". . . I'd rather be a man than a woman because a man would be free to ask anyone who appealed to him for dates. As is, I'm a respectable and respected community booster and divorcee—hate

that word. Have one grade school age child at home;
healthy, tired of having no sex or love life in the past
two and a half years, and can't do a damned thing
about it." This woman's unhappiness with her love life,
and her belief that she can do nothing about it, are
typical of divorced women, and to a lesser extent divorced men. For both men and women, the lack of a
love relationship and a decent sex life are serious obstacles to happiness. Although this may seem obvious,
it does not coincide with many people's image of the
newly divorced person. Particularly these days, there is
a general notion that divorce brings a wonderful
freedom and a very active sex and romantic life. We
may think that divorced men and women suddenly
have many dates, "screw around," have all sorts of excitement they had missed while married, and generally
find divorced life rewarding despite the burdens of
money and children and so on. This picture is probably
accurate for some divorced people—certainly some
lead a very active sex life and are very happy with the
love and romantic aspects of their lives—but it is not
true for most. There are singles bars, clubs for divorced people, special cruises, and so on; but apparently most divorced people still find it difficult to
meet people, or at least to meet the kind of people they
want to. All of the evidence is that during their divorced period, people tend to be lonely and unhappy.

Second Marriages

"The triumph of hope over experience"
—SAMUEL JOHNSON

Most divorced people remarry so that at some point
they form a new romantic relationship. By then, presumably, they have managed to overcome their loneliness and their lives should start looking up again. In
fact, we found that people who remarry are as happy
as those who are in their first marriages. There is no indication that second marriages are better, on average,
than first ones; but they are no worse. We have no reli-

able evidence on how those who remarry compare their first and second marriages. All we know is that people who are married only once say they are just as happy as but no happier than people who are married more than once.

On the other hand, there is no reason to believe that second marriages are the answer to marital bliss. A 1977 book by Leslie Westoff called *The Second Time Around* gives the impression that second marriages are even happier than first marriages. This conclusion is almost certainly more optimistic than justified. As Morton Hunt pointed out in a review of the book, Westoff spends almost no time discussing people whose second marriages also fail. Many do—second marriages fail even more than first ones, though not appreciably more. Obviously people who are staying in a marriage, whether it be first or second, give a rosier picture than people who are breaking up their marriage. Thus, talking only to people in second marriages that are working overestimates how good second marriages generally are.

To be fair, I should say that Westoff's finding probably represents the truth about people's attitudes toward a second marriage, especially soon after it has taken place. Most of these people were quite unhappy in their first marriage, and as we have seen, were extremely unhappy between marriages (the divorced are the unhappiest group). They must enter into a second marriage with great relief and optimism. They are older and supposedly wiser, they are determined not to make the same mistake again, but they have nevertheless met someone they care enough about to marry. The contrast with their first unhappy marriage and the bad time after it must make them especially happy at the beginning of the second marriage. And if after a while the second marriage continues to be good, they must be enormously grateful and relieved. It is not surprising that most of the people Westoff interviewed, people who were in a second marriage that was working (at least for the moment) described it in glowing terms. For them, it was a happy experience, particularly when contrasted with what came before.

Though Westoff probably overstates the happiness of second marriages, the evidence does indicate that they are very nearly as happy as first marriages. This is an interesting and important finding because of what it says about why marriages fail. It is sometimes suggested that marriages fail because some people are not cut out for marriage, are bad marriage partners, could not be happy in a marriage no matter with whom. This may be true, but it seems that it applies to only a small percentage of people. If a large number of first marriages failed because the people involved were bad partners, these people would also be unhappy in their second marriages; overall, second marriages, which would be made up mostly of people who were bad at marriage, would be much less happy than first ones. That is, the "good" marriage partners would get married and stay married; the "bad" marriage partners would end their first marriage, remarry, be unhappy and end that one, and either keep on marrying and getting divorced or just give up and stay single. But this is not what happens. The fact that people in second marriages are as happy as those in first marriages strongly indicates that marriage failures are not due mainly to some people being bad at marriage, but rather to complex factors involving the relationship between the two people, the stresses and strains of any long-term relationship, and a long list of other factors you can name as well as I can.

This is a good thing. It means that someone who has been divorced is not necessarily doomed to fail in a second marriage; it means that such a person is not a bad bet for marriage (no worse than someone who has not been married), and it means that the 40-50 percent of first marriages that end in divorce leave open the possibility that the individuals involved will be happy in a subsequent marriage. Since marriage is such an important element in general happiness for most people, this is surely one of our most reassuring findings. One failure, one poor choice, one relationship that does not work out, may cause considerable unhappiness, but it does not seem to reduce one's chance for finding happiness in marriage or in general. There is always a second chance, and if that does not work, a third. Perhaps a person experiences more moments or years of happiness if a first marriage is successful, but it is never too late to find the right partner, get married, and be as happy as anyone else.

Men versus Women in Second Marriages

Men and women respond somewhat differently to remarriage. Men seem to be, if anything, happier the second time—they find the marriage more romantic, say they are more in love, and that the love is more equal in the second marriage than it was in the first. This is not true for women.

We have seen that women are quite happy in their first marriage, that they are the happiest group in society. The second time, women are still reasonably happy, certainly much happier than single or divorced women, but not quite as well off as in a first marriage. This shows up in many ways. To begin with, fewer women say they are really happy with their second marriage. The percentage is still fairly high but it drops from three quarters who were happy with their first marriage to only two thirds in their second. Similarly, the women are less satisfied with their love life—fewer than two thirds are happy compared to over three quarters in a first marriage. What this means in round numbers is that an additional 10 percent of the women involved are less than fully happy with their second marriage.

On the question of reciprocal love, that most important element in connection with happiness, the pattern holds. Among first marriages, a surprisingly large number of people report that they are not in love with their spouse—almost one out of five men (18 percent) and one out of six women (15 percent). In second marriages it gets better for men (only 6 percent say they are not in love) and worse for women (up to 20 percent). Moreover, many of both sexes complain that the love relationship in the second marriage is totally or largely one-sided, with the other person loving more. But compared to first marriages, fewer men in second marriages have this complaint while more women do.

Women's diminished satisfaction with second marriages is reflected in a variety of specific symptoms and complaints. Again compared to women in their first marriages, a third more in their second marriage say that they experience anxiety attacks and that they are lonely; almost twice as many say that they sometimes feel they can't go on (a pretty extreme feeling), and that they do not receive enough recognition; and fully four times as many have at one time attempted suicide. All in all, they are clearly not as happy as a group as those in their first marriage.

As usual, we must not conclude the second marriage causes the unhappiness. Perhaps those who got divorced and remarried were less happy to begin with (i.e., were also unhappy in their first marriage—remember we have not followed particular individuals but merely asked people who were married either once or more than once).

There are many possible explanations. All we know is that for some reason men tell us that they are as happy or even happier in a second marriage, while women are substantially less likely to be happy than they are in a first marriage. Nevertheless, we must not forget that for both men and women, second marriages are happier than being single and much happier than remaining divorced.

Living Together

In addition to the people who are married, remarried, or divorced, there is a group of people who are "not quite married"—people who are living together in a romantic, sexual relationship not formalized by marriage vows. Most of these relationships, as far as we can tell, are not casual arrangements entered into on the spur of the moment simply for convenience, and most of them last for a considerable period of time—many months and often years.

It is difficult to find these people. Although there are undoubtedly hundreds of thousands of them in the country, they still constitute a very tiny percentage of the population. In a survey of the whole adult population you find so few people who are living together that their responses cannot be analyzed in detail. Magazine surveys, which reach a somewhat select audience population, uncovered a few more—between 2 and 5 percent of the people who reply are living together. This is still such a small number that one cannot be sure that their answers are representative. With this proviso, here is the little we know about people living together. (For convenience I shall call them LTs—living togethers.)

LTs differ from married people in several basic economic, social, and sexual characteristics. LTs are younger—30 percent under twenty-five, 75 percent under thirty-five; poorer—almost 50 percent with incomes under ten thousand dollars; less well educated—12 percent have less than a high school diploma. Married people are older and have more money and education; single people are even younger and much poorer, though they are better educated than the LTs.

Those who live together are much more likely than marrieds to live in an urban environment. Almost 20 percent live in a large city or a metropolis, compared to 10 percent of marrieds. And only half as many LTs live in rural areas as do marrieds. In this respect, LTs are very similar to singles. However, an interesting sidelight is that so many people who live in rural areas or small towns manage to live together without marriage. You might have thought—I did—that it would be difficult even today to maintain such an arrangement in a small community, but almost 30 percent of the LTs were living rural or small-town lives. This is much smaller than the percentage of marrieds, but it is still a substantial percentage.

One stereotype holds true: LTs lead more active

sexual lives than married people of about their age, and much more than singles. LTs have had more sex partners, by far, than any other group. Almost half of them have had at least seven partners, and the average is about five. In contrast, only a fifth of single people have had seven partners, and the average is about two or three. Married people have even fewer partners, averaging about two. Similarly, LTs engage in sex more frequently—about half of them having sexual intercourse three times a week or more (11 percent at least once a day), whereas among married people, the next most active group, only about a quarter have intercourse as often as three times a week and only 2 percent at least once a day. And as we would expect, this high activity does lead to greater satisfaction with sex. Almost 80 percent of the LTs said they were satisfied, compared to 70 percent of marrieds and 45 percent of singles.

Remember that we have a very small sample of LTs and our results, especially on complex questions like happiness, may not hold for a larger group. But we did find that people who live together say they are much happier than single people and almost as happy as marrieds. The contrast between LTs and singles is particularly dramatic between the ages of twenty and thirty for men, and from twenty-five on for women. In one survey 65 percent of women LTs said they were very or moderately happy while only 55 percent of single women were this happy; and only 10 percent of the LTs were quite unhappy, compared to 15 percent of the single women. These differences are greater than they may seem: consider that half again as many singles were unhappy as were LTs. On the other hand, LTs were generally somewhat less happy than married people. The differences were small, and were not entirely consistent, but in most studies, married people were the happiest, followed closely by LTs, with singles far behind. The reasons are probably to be found in the way that living together resembles marriage. Like marrieds, LTs are less likely to be lonely than single people; those who are married or living together have a regular sex partner and thus are more likely to have active, satisfying sex lives than single people, and couples living together are better off financially than single people, though less well off than married people. In other words, although living together is not identical to marriage, it is more similar to it than being single; and to the extent that having a stable, long-term love relationship brings happiness, LTs and married people should benefit from this.

Although these findings are encouraging for living together as an alternative to marriage, they hardly demonstrate that the former is associated with more happiness, or that living together solves any of the problems often found in legal marriage. In addition, living together poses some problems that marriage seems to solve or at least do better with.

Although LTs are somewhat more satisfied with sex than are marrieds, LTs are less happy with love. At first glance this is surprising. LTs are younger than marrieds, and we know that at least among married men satisfaction with love declines as time goes on. There is, too, a "romantic" aspect to living together that marriage rarely has in our society. Despite these factors, married people report being slightly more satisfied with their love relationship than those who are living together. Moreover, LTs are much more likely than marrieds to say that they are in an unequal love relationship, in which one partner loves more than the other. Sixty percent of married people feel they have a reciprocal love relationship—not a very high percentage—but only 48 percent of LTs feel their love is reciprocal. In this respect, the male LTs are much worse off than the women, with only 43 percent of the men, compared to 53 percent of the women, thinking the relationship is equal. Among those who do not think it is equal, almost all of the men say that their partner loves more than they do, while women are divided about evenly between those who think the other loves more and those who think they love more. Finally, when asked how satisfied they are with their romantic relationship in general, only 74 percent of the LTs are moderately or very happy compared to an impressive 80 percent of the marrieds.

Of course, all of this is mixed up with age, attitudes toward marriage, income, career, and expectations. People who live together, even in our relatively liberal times, are different from those who choose to get married. Perhaps they choose to live together without marriage because they are "not ready" for marriage—too young or, more likely, too unsure about their love or their relationship. Presumably the latter would suggest that when they did choose to marry, they would be more sure and the relationship would (we can hope) be even better. We do not know enough to be certain why LTs are less happy than married people. Definitive answers will have to await a comprehensive study of marriage and alternatives. We have too little data, too few cases of LTs, to be certain of our results. For the moment, all we can say is that based on the information we have, people who live together are much happier than single people and only slightly less happy than married people.

We have looked at four groups of people. In ascending order of happiness, they are divorced people who have not remarried, single people who have never married, unmarried people living together, and married people. Two facts stand out from all the information we have. The first is that there is a large "happiness gap" between people living without a partner and people living with one. Partnership, whether or not it is legalized by a wedding ceremony, is associated with much more happiness than solitude. All the corny jokes and bitter novels notwithstanding, all the real frictions that are caused by living close to another person notwithstanding, people need partners. We are gregarious animals and partnership makes us happy.

There is, however, a troubling undercurrent in the stream of married happiness. Time and again the survey data and interviews reveal that many women are deeply troubled by some aspects of marriage. The next chapter deals with marriage, women, and freedom.

6. *Women, Freedom, and Marriage*

"I would change places with a single woman . . ."
—SURVEY RESPONSE

The traditional view of marriage—memorialized in countless stale, silly jokes—is that every woman wants it but that men have to be convinced. The woman must lure, capture, sometimes trick the man into marriage because he wants to remain free while she wants to settle down. That notion, never especially accurate, is particularly misguided nowadays. The evidence is that women, much more than men, are in conflict about marriage—not only about the value of marriage itself, but also about the nature of men's and women's roles in marriage. This conflict is a constant theme of letters and interviews collected during our research on happiness. A young woman envies her friend because ". . . she is married and has a newborn baby and they live in a large, very old house full of antiques." For each statement of this kind, we have five or more that say the opposite—a married woman wants to be single, envying a single friend ". . . because her time is her own. She can travel and go places whenever she wants to. When you're married and have children life is never your own . . ." Marriage does bring happiness—married women are happier than single ones—but many women want out. Why?

Naturally, many of these women are unhappy because they feel they have chosen the wrong man, or because the marriage has not worked out well. Both sexes have these complaints and many marriages—almost half—therefore end in divorce. When for one reason or another incompatible people do not get divorced, they often live with considerable or even desperate unhappiness. But it is much more than this that is bothering married women. Many of those who complain about marriage claim that they are happily married, that they love their husbands and children. For example, the woman quoted above added: "Don't get me wrong. I love my family very much and they are the center of my life. But if I had it to do over again, I wouldn't get married."

One woman, a schoolteacher of thirty-four who earns an excellent income, may have summed up many of the specific complaints shared by large numbers of women. She told us: "I feel I would enjoy my life exactly the way it is minus the husband. How do I know this could be true? This week my husband is away and what a joyous week it has been. There is no one to constantly tell, or suggest what I should do and how it should be done. There is no one around who sits on his ass after his day's work is done while I'm still working after my day's work is done. This week I feel as competent at home as I do at work. This week I enjoy playing with the kids because there is no negative feeling around me. This week everyone does his share of work, not just the slaves. This week the tension is gone. This week I can finish my work at school before coming home rather than doing it at home after I've made a decent meal, and after the kids and I have done the dishes and cleaned the kitchen, and after I have finished the wash, etc. etc. etc. I can go to bed when I am tired with no guilt feelings. This week I do not feel like a workhorse, a money machine, a maid, and I'm not. This week I feel like a complete person. Would I marry again? No, because I know what next week will hold when he comes home again."

This litany of complaint is echoed by many others. The specific points in them are less important than the theme that runs through them all—freedom to be a whole person, to be treated as an equal, independent entity. Married women of all ages, all economic levels, working and nonworking, say they want more freedom, and that is the central theme of their dissatisfaction with marriage.

It is ironic that what women find most lacking in marriage is exactly what men are supposed to be concerned about—their own freedom. In most instances this is not sexual freedom, but something much more basic—freedom to do what they want, to pursue careers or travel, to find themselves as people, to express their feelings, to grow. Women find marriage restricts and limits these freedoms, even when they love their husbands and are generally happy. Here is a woman of thirty-one who says she is neither happy nor unhappy, who is a secretary and homemaker who has two children and a good income and who writes: "I would change places with a single woman, as I feel very strongly that my children and husband, who sometimes do enrich my life, are very demanding upon the *me* which I have come to know. I would remain single and childless and work and more thoroughly enjoy myself." She is not especially unhappy with her husband or her marriage—in fact, she says they are both pretty good and give her considerable happiness. Similarly, her sex and love lives are pretty good, she enjoys her children, and has a very happy social life with friends. Yet she wishes very much that she had never married and thinks she would be much happier if she hadn't. It would give her more freedom to express herself.

Another woman, this one forty-nine years old, told us that her love life and marriage were quite good—made her moderately happy. She has a full-time job at which she earns good money, and she is moderately happy with her life in general. "I would like a more exciting life. My husband is a good man, but his interests and excitements are not the same as mine. . . . I want to jump out of this cocoon." And a twenty-six-year-old with no children and a full-time job that pays more than fifteen thousand dollars: "I would change lives with a single woman who is about my age. She can progress in her career without thinking of how it will affect a husband."

And a woman of thirty with two children, working full-tme and moderately happy with love, sex, marriage, and just about everything else: "I'd like to change places with a single female with a life in which she finds time for self-oriented activities as well as work, etc., someone who is free to go out and meet all types of people, with responsibilities based solely on her life as *an individual*, not as part of a family, couple, etc."

Although the specific ways these women state their complaints differ somewhat, it seems clear that they are feeling hemmed in even by reasonably happy marriages. They may care about their husbands and children, but they feel that they cannot act as independent people, cannot express their own personalities, cannot be themselves because they are defined and limited by their families. The complaints are by no means limited to women involved in the women's movement; it is obvious that marriage is much more restricting for women than for men. This has been discussed at length in books from *Middlemarch* to *The Feminine Mystique* and *The Female Eunuch*. The simple fact is that in our society women are much more likely to be defined in terms of their husbands than the other way around. Is it any wonder that a married woman thinks of herself in terms of the family rather than as an independent person when her name is his, she is introduced as his wife or as Mrs. somebody, when she can travel on his passport but he cannot travel on hers, when her income doesn't count for getting a loan even though she has a good job? Many of these things are changing, but they change slowly and, in any case, the women we interviewed have lived during a period before the change began.

Some women seem to have escaped by choosing an entirely independent life. Earlier I quoted from a letter from a wonderful woman of seventy-nine, a physician who seems to have led a very full life even though she never married. Here are her views on marriage: "On the whole, I would not change lives with any other person. Whatever limitation of freedom I met was incidental to free choices I had made. I have had much joy in travel. Human relationships mean a great deal to me. My relationships have been few but very deep. I cannot endure the superficial social life most people live. While I should have liked to have been married, when I compare my life now with those of most women who have given their lives to their family, I think I am happier than most at this age. If they have given their lives to their family, they are now widowed and their children are grown up and gone, and they have made inadequate preparation for a solitary old age. Since I have lived always rather solitary, it is no problem for me. . . ."

She sounds happy and satisfied with her life and the life she has led. But hers is an extreme solution. She gave up romance and sex (she had no sexual partners) and family. Few people, men or women, would be willing to do the same.

One woman chose divorce and is quite happy despite her lack of a love relationship. She says: "It is such a relief to be free. Believe me, with all the problems, I'm delighted to be free to be me, to be out of a situation where I couldn't be, free to do what I want, with the limitations of the community maybe, but freer than I ever was before. And that's what makes me happy now and what made me unhappy before." Yet even she complains bitterly about the absence of love in her life. For many women marriage and family are binding, but the alternative is loneliness and often frustration.

The Joys of Marriage and Family

I do not want to give the impression that most women prefer to remain single. All of the evidence is that married women are happier than single ones or divorced ones. This is true at all ages and for all economic and educational levels. It is true for women who work and for women who do not work. (By the same token, educated working women do not escape the conflict we have been discussing.) Almost all of the people who said they were very happy attributed this, at least in part, to a long-term romantic relationship involving marriage and a family. Moreover, many of those who were most miserable blamed it on the *loss* of a husband or wife. One woman who wrote had led a wonderful life until her husband died. She became terribly unhappy for several years. Just before answering our questionnaire, she "began seeing and lived with a wonderful man, married that wonderful man, and reached a level of happiness I never thought possible." It may sound as if this is a very dependent woman who cannot get along on her own and needs a man to take care of her. Not at all: she has a good job, works hard, and makes a decent living on her own, has had quite a few sexual partners, tried marijuana and strongly believes that her life has meaning and direction. Make of this what you will, but she does not seem to me to be a weak, dependent person. Yet for her, happiness seems to require marriage, or some equivalent, and independence is not a critical issue, either because she maintains it anyway or because she does not care about it.

It seems clear that for many married women, probably a large majority, a good marriage brings happiness because of the love and care, the security and attention, the sharing and support, and the joy obtained from the happiness and success of husband and children. None of this requires that women give up their independence or be any less themselves; and some women manage to experience the joys of marriage without doing so. Others probably find happiness in marriage at the expense of some independence, and perhaps they would say the sacrifice is worthwhile. There are others, however, who may or may not get some happiness from marriage, but they think that the price in terms of freedom is too high.

One thing that seems to help is work; married women who work are happier. Actually this may be an oversimplification. In fact, working and nonworking women *say* that they are equally happy. This is complicated by the fact that working women tend to be somewhat younger, have fewer children, and be better educated. But no matter how we break down their answers, work does not seem to have much effect on how happy they say they are.

On the other hand, this is one instance in which more detailed analyses may be illuminating. One difficulty with asking people how happy they are is that their answers may to some extent be influenced by their perceptions of how happy they should be. According to our cultural traditions, a woman who is married to a good man with a good income, who has a good house and good children, should be happy. This tradition is changing, but most women still seem to feel that there is something wrong with them if they are not happy in such a situation. Betty Friedan points out in *The Feminine Mystique* that many married women who found themselves unhappy even though they "had everything a woman could want" blamed themselves, decided that something was missing inside them, rather than looking for a cause in society or in their marriage.

In any case, people do rate their happiness in part according to their image of themselves and their situation, and married women may do this more than others. This may explain why working and nonworking women rate themselves equally happy, and we looked for other evidence on how happy they were. In particular, we looked at responses to other questions that are usually thought to be related to happiness and well-being. For example, if you knew that someone had tried to commit suicide five times in the last year, you would probably be skeptical if she also said that she had been very happy during that period. Similarly, if someone has constant headaches, cannot sleep, feels nervous all the time, and often thinks she cannot go on, one has a right to wonder whether she really is as marvelously happy as she says.

Our survey therefore asked people whether they had recently experienced any of a long list of symptoms. We included just about everything that is usually considered psychologically related—from headaches, insomnia, and nightmares to ulcers and constipation, from constant worry to feeling lonely. Almost all of these were found to correlate with happiness—people who had the symptoms were less happy and less optimistic about life. Thus, it may be possible to use these symptoms as an independent indication of how happy someone is, separate from what they say about their level of happiness.

Married women who do not work are much more likely to have these kinds of symptoms than working women. The most important symptoms are: insomnia, nightmares, constant worry and anxiety, chronic diarrhea and/or constipation, tiring easily, trouble concentrating, crying spells, often feeling lonely, and feelings of worthlessness. For example, employed wives are less anxious and worried (28 versus 46 percent), less lonely (26 versus 44 percent), and less likely to feel worthless (24 versus 41 percent) than housewives. A working woman is less likely to feel lonely, to cry a lot, to feel she cannot go on, and to feel worthless. This suggests that the working women are in fact happier even though they do not differ in how they describe their happiness. It does not mean that working women are always happier than those who do not work—obviously there is a lot of variation, with some married women being very happy not to work and some working women miserable. All it suggests is that for women in general, at this moment in history, being married and working seems to produce greater happiness than being married without working.

In this context, it is important to note that we do not find similar differences in the frequency with which symptoms occur between women with or without children, among groups of men, between single and married people in general, and so on. In other words, the greatest incidence of symptoms seems to be concentrated among married, non-working women.

Thus, three facts regarding marriage and women emerge: married women are happier than single women; married women who have a paying job appear to be happier than those who do not have one; but among both those with and without jobs, many women feel that marriage is restricting. It seems as if this concern with freedom and lack of it is due to the conflict between traditional roles of husbands and wives and the more recent view that the roles should be largely equivalent. Even working wives often are expected to make dinner and assume major responsibility for children and so on. While this role of mother and homemaker pleases many women (including some who have full-time jobs), it makes others feel restricted and even mistreated. With more and more women working, and with attitudes toward marriage and work changing, these dissatisfactions may disappear or decline in the coming years. For the moment we have the paradox that married women are our happiest group and yet they often are unhappy with the lack of freedom they think their marriage produces.

7. Youth and Age

"Grow up as soon as you can. It pays. The only time you really live fully is from thirty to sixty."
—HERVEY ALLEN, ANTHONY ADVERSE

Most important characteristics of people usually remain stable throughout their lives. We stay the same sex (barring trans-sexual operations), maintain about the same height, have the same skin color and national origin, may remain at about the same financial situation, work at the same kind of job, and even stay in the same marital status for much of our lives. But age changes constantly. Growing older is the one guaranteed result of living, which, as someone said, is better than the alternative. Because age is so basic and so changing, it is almost always examined in studies of happiness. As a result, we have a large amount of information on how age and happiness are related.

Perceptions of Different Ages

Before considering the actual relationship between age and happiness, it is interesting to note that most people have definite conceptions of what life is like at various ages, especially regarding happiness. When people are asked which period of life is happiest (*for others*), they generally agree that old age and adolescence are the worst. Old age is seen as an unhappy time because of the poverty in which many of the aged live, because friends and family have moved away or died, because retirement is boring, and, of course, because your body has deteriorated, you are likely to be sick, and you are going to die soon. As for adolescence, we know that it is a difficult period in which there are too many crucial decisions to be made. The adolescent is not independent, yet cannot count on his parents to take care of him. Social, sexual, and career problems abound. Psychoanalysts would add that adolescence is a time during which people are trying to come to terms with their own freedom and their sometimes frightening impulses, are trying to decide just who they are (the famous adolescent identity crisis), and are torn by conflicting values and motives.

In our youth-oriented culture, one might think that the period of young adulthood would be the one most people would see as happiest. Strangely, the happiest time is thought to be middle age, roughly the years from thirty-five to fifty-five. Even though the phrase "middle-aged" is often said with scorn, even though people resist becoming middle-aged (the perpetual twenty-nine-year-olds), middle age is considered not only the prime of life but also the happiest time of life. Why? Perhaps because by one's midthirties, one has gotten past the traumas of adolescence and the struggles of early adulthood while the illnesses, weaknesses, and fear of old age are still far away. Whatever the reason, we tend to perceive middle age

as the happiest time of life—for others. As I shall discuss in a moment, our perceptions of our own lives and
the actual relationship between age and happiness are
another story.

In addition to ratings of overall happiness, people
have notions about the opportunities for happiness that
are available at various ages. These are not all consistent with ratings of happiness. Adolescence, for example, that siege of anxiety and pain for so many, is seen
as the time when one has most chances for fun and
happiness, possibly because it is a time of little responsibility. The teen-ager is seen as a person free to do
pretty much what he or she wants without the restrictions imposed by the necessity of earning a living or
deep emotional or legal entanglements. The teen-ager
is also seen as largely free from the burden of "acting
like an adult." Many rules of behavior that apply to
older members of society are relaxed for adolescents.
From adults, we expect a steady job, stable sex and
family life, participation in the affairs of society, and
generally responsible behavior. (We don't always get
all of this, but we expect it.) In contrast, the adolescent is free not to work, to have no fixed goals, to engage in wild or unusual sex practices, to dress sloppily
or strangely, to become involved in odd religions, fads,
or cults, or simply to abandon all cares and hitchhike
around the world. Their parents may object, the neighbors may talk, but the kids can be forgiven or even admired for behavior that would not be acceptable from
an adult. And so—people seem to think—the adolescent has many opportunities to have fun and to be
happy.

Young adulthood and middle age are seen as providing similar opportunities for fun and happiness (though
fewer than adolescence), and old age is seen as offer-
ing many fewer opportunities. The two middle periods
apparently are perceived as having the advantages of
better position in the world, more money and independence, but the disadvantages of responsibilities and ties
that prevent people from pursuing their interests. Also,
people in these middle years are seen as more conser-

vative than adolescents, not politically, but personally—less willing to take chances, try new things, and
so on. In old age, we assume there are fewer opportunities because people are poorer, in less good health,
and are also the most conservative.

It is interesting to note that middle age is perceived
as being the happiest period despite the fact that adolescence is seen as giving the most opportunities to be
happy. Apparently, we agree with George Bernard
Shaw that youth is too wonderful to be wasted on the
young. We think youth offers the chances but that
young people do not or cannot take advantage of them;
whereas middle-aged people, who have fewer opportunities, manage to use more of them and be happier.
The reason is not freedom (since adolescents are the
most free) but that older people seem to know better
what they want and how to get it.

Age and Happiness

What people think about the happiness of others does
not always square with what they think of their own.
The same group of people who offered their perceptions
of others' happiness, described their own opportunities
for fun and happiness and their own general level of
happiness. Even though they saw big differences among
the various age groups when they looked at other
people, it turned out that there were no differences in
their ratings of themselves. The young, the middle-aged,
and the old considered themselves equally happy. Not
only that, but they said that they had equal opportunities for fun and happiness. The only difference among
the groups was that the adolescents said that they had a
greater *desire* for fun and happiness, that it meant more
to them and they pursued it more avidly. Despite our
perceptions of major differences among age groups, all
of the studies of happiness have found that there is little
or no relationship between age and happiness. The
middle years are not the happiest—they are the same as
any other. And most strikingly, old age (sixty-five and

older) does not differ appreciably from any other period in terms of average happiness.

Although there are no overall differences in happiness, we do find some interesting and perhaps crucial differences. Naturally, there are some changes that occur with age. As people get older, their health worsens and they are less happy with this aspect of their lives. This seems obvious, but a fascinating sidelight is that this decline in satisfaction with health is steady and gradual from about twenty to forty-five and then stops. From the age of forty-five on, people do not report any noticeable change in the extent to which health is a problem or a source of unhappiness. Certainly, their actual health gets worse on average; but their happiness with it does not. Perhaps this is because in middle age people tend to worry about even small illnesses, while in old age they get used to minor aches and pains and worry only about things that are serious. Whatever the reason, a large random sample of the American population said that satisfaction with health was about the same at forty-five as at sixty-five.

Many other aspects of life improve with age. Satisfaction with one's job increases up to age thirty-five, then levels off. Presumably this is because up to that age people are settling into their jobs, getting established, and from then on they tend to stay in the same field and already know if they are successful or unsuccessful, enjoy it or do not. Although people may continue to improve their position after thirty-five, the big fights may be largely over.

Financial situation, feelings of recognition and success, and a sense of personal growth also improve with age up to a point and level off during middle age. Similarly, satisfaction with friends, love, and marriage improve from adolescence through young adulthood and then drop slightly, while satisfaction with sex is very low in adolescence, increases up to age twenty-five and shows little change thereafter until it begins to drop gradually after fifty-five. (The decline after fifty-five is accounted for mainly by the increase in the number of widows and widowers; people who are married are almost as happy with their sex lives at sixty-five as they are at thirty five.) In contrast, religion and other spiritual feelings become a more important source of satisfaction after thirty-five and continue to increase in importance right up to old age.

Taken together, these trends may explain why the various age groups differ so little in overall happiness. Factors that are good at one time are less good at another, but at any given period the average of all factors is about the same. You may be less happy with sex in old age but happier with religion, less happy with friends in middle age than in young adulthood but happier with your job, and so on. Taken together, they add up to just about the same amount of happiness at any time, even though the sources and the mixtures are slightly different.

Old Age

Although there are no differences in the average happiness reported by age groups, a somewhat different pattern emerges in old age. The sixty-five-and-up group tends to greater extremes. More people in this period than in any other say they are very unhappy but more also say that they are very happy. For some reason, this time of life seems to be either very good or very bad to a greater extent than other times.

The relatively large number of very unhappy old people is easier to explain. It results at least in part from actual misfortunes that are more likely to befall the elderly than younger people. In general, health does not show up as one of the most important factors in happiness, but this is because most people are in good health whatever their age. To a greater extent than one might think, people get used to minor illnesses or disabilities. They adapt to frailty, to weak kidneys, or an ulcer. Such illnesses have a constant effect on what you can eat and do, how much or how fast you can travel, on the life style you are able to lead. But people seem to manage to be just as happy with these chronic conditions as with perfect health. In the surveys, many people with poor health say they are very happy, and very few consider health a major factor in their happiness.

But really serious illness or disability is another story. Some people may adapt to it and be reasonably happy. Most people cannot. Grave disabilities or terminal or possibly terminal illness have profound negative effects on their lives and make happiness extremely difficult to find. And, of course, older people tend to have more serious illnesses than younger ones. Even though concerns about health do not increase markedly after forty-five, the rate of serious illness does; and this accounts in part for the higher percentage of older people who are very unhappy.

More important than one's own aches and pains are the illnesses and deaths that strike friends and relatives, and these occur much more often as you get older. One of the saddest things about old age, which many people mention, is the feeling that all the people you were close to have died or are sick. A woman of seventy-one who says she is in fine health herself and otherwise quite content with her life says: "But I am one of the lucky ones and most of my friends have not been lucky. They are almost all gone now. Even though I have some young people who visit me and are friendly, I feel lonely for those I used to know who were my age." And a seventy-eight-year-old man who is still active in his own company, clearly with a great zest for life and with lots of energy, told us: "I keep busy with the business which I still find just as much fun as ever. My main complaint is that there's no one around any more. There used to be a group of us who worked together and would get together all the time, and they are all dead or too sick to get out." If you live to a very old age, you will be older than everyone around you and will undoubtedly witness the deaths of those you love—siblings, spouses, and even your own children. At any age, the death of someone close is difficult and painful; in old age you are more likely to experience these deaths and they will leave you more alone. A woman of sixty-eight who had lost her husband four years ago wrote that it was the worst thing that had ever happened to her and her life had been unhappy ever since. "He left me wonderfully provided for financially, I have three loving children who visit me often, and I have many friends. But life will never be the same again and I wish it had been me instead of him." A very sad and unhappy woman of eighty-four said that she thought it was "wonderful" that she had lived so long and was so healthy. Yet "I don't see the sense of it. My husband of forty years is gone; my two sisters and brother are gone; two of my children are gone; everyone I cared about except only my youngest daughter is gone and she lives in Ohio [the woman is in Arizona.] I always thought people was what I lived for and now there isn't anyone and each time one of them went, I didn't think I could stand it. Well, I stood it well enough, but now I'm all alone. . . ." Young people tend to think that their own health will be the most serious difficulty of old age, but many older people say that the poor health of others is their greatest source of unhappiness.

A second reason for the greater incidence of extreme unhappiness among old people is a dramatic change for the worse in the social structure of their lives. Many older people are widowed. If a married woman lives to seventy, her chance of being widowed is better than 50 percent; if she lives to seventy-five (as most women do), the odds of her being widowed are better than three to one. It is lonely to be widowed. As we mentioned earlier, married people are happier than unmarried, and widows and widowers are among the least happy groups in society.

Income is a third factor contributing to the extremes of unhappiness among the aged. A high percentage of older people fall into the lowest income groups. They live on Social Security payments, which are considerably below poverty level, or depend in part on fixed incomes from savings and pensions that are whittled away by inflation. It is bad enough to be poor when you are young, have opportunities ahead of you, have energy and good health, and also have not gotten used to having more. But it is presumably much worse to be poor when you are older, few opportunities loom ahead, and you need more comfort and care. It is especially difficult to live on little money when you are accustomed to more. As with everything else, we are more sensitive to changes in our lives than to steady situations. Thus, older people often find their poverty not only difficult in itself, but also humiliating and demeaning. For example, one elderly couple sent in separate answers to a questionnaire but wrote a letter jointly. Among other things, they said: "It is very hard to get used to not having money. We never were rich, but we had a good income all the time we were married. Now that we are retired [he is seventy-two, she sixty-eight,] we have time to do all the things we put off or couldn't do before, but there's no money for anything. We have to watch every penny, just like we were unemployed or on welfare. It is awful when you are used to buying decent meat and not having to count every nickel, to have to look for specials and make sure you don't spend an extra penny. We feel as if all those years of work are forgotten now and we are like bums."

Retirement

Retirement is a fourth factor in the unhappiness of older people, but it works in complicated ways. For years the common belief in American society was that retirement was something to look forward to—"the golden years" when the children were grown and Mom and Dad could rest, relax, visit with grandchildren, take up hobbies. Recently this image of retirement has changed drastically. Now it is widely believed that retirement is bad for people. We hear sad descriptions of people who were vigorous, active, and youthful until the day they retired, when they quickly deteriorated. The notion is that work and activity and having a place in society keep you young, and that retirement kills.

This is not the place to argue which of these images of retirement is correct. There is probably some truth in both. The effect of retirement on happiness, however, is much weaker than many suppose. The reported happiness levels of people in the later years, including a great many who have retired, is no lower than in any other group. Moreover, studies of retirement have shown that many people respond to it very well and actually do enjoy life more after retiring than before. The fact of the matter is that many people do not especially like their jobs, or are tired of them; for most of them, retirement is a relief. They do not feel they have been "put out to pasture" but rather that they have been given an opportunity to enjoy the good things in life rather than breaking their backs on a hateful job. Then there are many who have specific interests they want to pursue. Indeed, these are the ones who seem to do best after retirement. The evidence suggests that, as supposed, it is good to "keep busy." But a nine-to-five job is not necessarily the best way to do so. Retirement is not necessarily a death certificate; it does not necessarily lead to a decline in health, vitality, or happiness; it can often have positive and beneficial effects.

On the other hand, there is little question that retirement does have disastrous effects on some people. One study found that 15 percent of those who retire respond very badly. This 15 percent probably includes many of the relatively large number of older people who say they are very unhappy. Again, a change matters more than a steady state; and if this particular change is seen as bad, it may produce real misery.

Given all of these problems and especially the awareness of approaching death, it is hardly surprising that we find a substantial number of older people who are very unhappy. What is surprising is that the average happiness level of old people is so high. Perhaps this is a tribute to our amazing ability as a species to adapt to difficult situations and make the best of them; or perhaps old age has compensations that make up for these other difficulties.

Happy Older People

Now let us turn to the other end of the scale, the high percentage of older people who say they are very happy. Why should the oldest group have more people who are very happy than any other age group? The data that have been collected do not give us a definite answer to this question, but there are some hints.

First, satisfaction with life increases with age. The difference between satisfaction and happiness is not totally clear, but it appears that satisfaction involves acceptance, a willingness to say, this is OK, I do not need or want more, it is a good life. Happiness implies more than this. It implies a more active enjoyment of life, and many people say they have one without the other. In particular, many older people say they are satisfied but not especially happy; whereas younger people often say the opposite. However, the two are obviously closely related. Satisfaction is a big first step toward happiness. That is, if you feel satisfied with life, it probably causes you to rate your happiness higher also, even though they are not identical feelings.

For reasons that are obscure, older people sometimes say that they are more optimistic about life than younger people. This is very surprising, given that young people have their whole lives ahead of them while older people do not. One wonders what they are being optimistic about. Yet there they are—very optimistic about the future. Almost 80 percent of older women, for example, say they are optimistic, compared to only 65 percent of the youngest group.

This optimism may also be tied up with a sense of satisfaction about life. Most of the important decisions have been made; whatever accomplishments, relationships, successes, recognition, loves, and so on that are going to be yours have occurred; and older people look back at their lives and look at their present lives with what can only be called a philosophical view that most younger people lack. Of course older people could look back and say, "How terrible my life was. What mistakes I made. How little I did. . . ." Undoubtedly some do this and they are the unhappy ones. But a large majority seem to take the opposite view—to say, "Whatever I did, I did it, and it wasn't too bad, I am more or less satisfied with it, and I am pretty satisfied with my life now."

In relation to this, it is worth noting that older people differ considerably from younger people in how often they think about happiness. Once again, the average amount of time spent is about the same, but older people seem to split into two very different types. There are a large number (50 percent) who think about happiness at least every day while another large group (25 percent) almost never think about happiness at all. In contrast, among younger people these two extremes are much less common: most younger people think about happiness regularly but not daily. Many older people seem simply to put happiness out of their minds, perhaps because it seems irrelevant to them. A larger group, perhaps because they have more time to reflect, think about happiness daily. We sometimes hear that the young are so worried about being happy, so concerned with seeking happiness, that it interferes with their lives and even with finding happiness. Once more, common notions appear to be wrong. Older people think at least as much about happiness as younger people, and this thinking is unrelated to how happy one is. It is probably not good to think about happiness too much, to question constantly whether you are happy; but even once a day does not seem to be too much. Both older and younger people who think daily about happiness are just as happy as those who think about it less often. Just as thinking about how good a meal tastes or how wonderful a trip is does not necessarily make them less enjoyable, so thinking about happiness does not seem to reduce it if it is there.

Religion plays a larger role in the lives of older people than younger people. This is partly because people tend to become more religious as they get older. It is also due, in part, to a continual trend in our country over the past fifty years for each generation to be less religious than the previous one. Thus, people who are now in their sixties or older belong to a generation that was more religious throughout their lives than later groups. This greater religiousness extends to non-religious philosophical and ethical beliefs as well. Older people have greater confidence in their guiding values, are more certain that life has meaning and direction, and generally seem to place greater emphasis on spiritual values than younger people.

Considering all age groups, religiousness is not related to happiness. Those who are religious, believe in God, and in an afterlife are no happier than those who are not religious and do not believe. We shall return to this in a later chapter. For now, the important point is that the considerable happiness in later years is not due to any great extent to religion. Religious belief is certainly very important for many people, but others are just as happy with few or no religious feelings.

However, the full range of religious, spiritual, and ethical beliefs does seem to be closely related to happiness, and taken together they may be an important factor related to happiness among older people. As we shall discuss in another chapter, people who have confidence in their guiding values and who think that life has meaning tend to be considerably happier than those who do not. Whereas religious beliefs are usually impersonal, these guiding values are directly related to the individual. If *your* values are correct, if *your* life has meaning, you are more likely to be happy than if you have no values and think your life meaningless. Since older people are more likely to hold these beliefs, this is probably one element in the large number of older people who are very happy.

Age and Expectations

One of the reasons that age makes little difference and that older people are, if anything, happier than younger ones, may be expectations. One theory of happiness is that it consists of getting what you expect or perhaps a little more. If you expect very little, but get it, you will be happier than someone who gets less than he expects. Personally, I am not convinced that this is the whole story. If only expectations mattered, the poor in India should be as happy as the rich in the United States—in fact happier, because the Indian must expect very little and is rarely disappointed while the rich American probably expects a great deal and is often disappointed.

Yet expectations clearly do matter, and they relate very well to our findings about the effects of age on happiness. Surely, the young have very high expectations, especially about happiness. People in their teens and twenties have been told all their lives that these are the best years, that everything is ahead of them, that they have all the opportunities. Even they agree that they have the most opportunities for fun and excitement and happiness. When it turns out that they are not deliriously happy all the time, they have all sorts of problems dealing with life and with themselves; it must be discouraging and disappointing.

In contrast, almost everyone has a dimmer view of old age. As we saw earlier, people expect old age to be a time of unhappiness. They expect to be less healthy than they were when they were younger, they expect to have less energy, they expect to worry about death, and so on. We think we will be past our prime, over the hill. Our expectations for happiness are certainly lower. When it turns out that old age is not as bad as we feared, that our health is pretty good (if we are lucky), that retirement is restful rather than boring, that many of our personal problems are solved or no longer relevant, it must be a great relief. And so when someone asks us if we are happy, we tend to say yes because our actual state is so much better than we expected it to be.

Of course, this view of the finding suggests that older people are not *really* as happy as younger people, they just think they are. But what does this mean? If you feel happy, you are happy—that's all we mean by the term. If relief at not being miserable makes you feel good, then you are happy; if disappointment at life's being worse than you expected makes you feel bad, then you are unhappy. Perhaps the number of exciting times, the moments of joy, the experiences that bring intense pleasure may be fewer in old age than in youth; but perhaps these are replaced by more moments of other kinds of satisfactions; and perhaps the fewer moments of pleasure are savored more and mean more than in youth. All we can say is that older people say they are as happy as younger ones, and every indication is that they mean what they say. Whatever the explanation—lower expectations, a somewhat different mix of pleasure and excitement versus peace of mind and satisfaction—this is an encouraging finding. After all, each of us is planning to grow older.

Age and Sources of Happiness

It is interesting to look at what people of various ages say about how to find happiness. As people get older, their views on how to achieve this quest change substantially. Edward Scott asked a number of children, teen-agers, university students, and adults a series of questions about happiness. Two of the things he asked were these: How does one go about seeking happiness? and Describe the happiest event you can recall.

In answer to the first question, the youngest group—eleven and twelve years old—talked mostly about interpersonal factors: having friends, helping friends, and going to parties. He quotes one girl as saying: "The things that make me happy are when we go to the movies and when we get to have art school. But most of all what makes me happy is when I get to have one of my girl friends come and spend the night with me." But the children's happiest recollections tended to involve gifts or birthdays as much as social occasions. (Getting a bicycle or a horse rated especially high.)

Teen-agers have shifted the focus almost entirely inward. Mental attitude, having an optimistic outlook, and knowing yourself are seen as the keys to happiness, with friendships a distant second. "Happiness must first be found within yourself," according to the teen-agers. However, as might be expected, romance plays the most important role in happiest events, with achievement, new experiences, and experience of the self coming next.

University students make a distinction between attitude (taking it easy, letting happiness come) and knowing themselves, both of which rank very high, with friends a close third. Clearly, they ask for more and require more for happiness. The happiest events involve romance, friends, personal achievements.

Adults put the stress squarely on their own attitudes—taking it easy, having peace of mind, acceptance. Friends, romance, achievement, work are mentioned very little. However, marriage and the birth of children are by far the most common events considered happiest.

In other words, all groups except children talk about internal attitudes rather than what goes on outside, but there is a change of emphasis at different ages. The teen-agers and college-aged people think a great deal about knowing themselves and being themselves. As Erik Erikson and others have noted, this is the time of the identity crisis. Friends, romance, and achievement are important, but resolving internal conflicts seems crucial. In contrast, the older people do not mention self-knowledge. Rather, they stress attitudes and acceptance of the world.

Perhaps this shift is a key to understanding happiness at various ages. Adolescents must face internal struggles. Although life seems simpler in many ways, responsibilities fewer, opportunities for fun and excitement many, the adolescent is often troubled by internal conflicts that make it difficult to enjoy what is available. Later, people have either resolved their conflicts or learned better to live with them, but then, alas, the freedom is less and some of the opportunities gone. Thus, overall, it works about the same at each age— not that people find happiness in exactly the same activities or same ways at all ages, but that the balance between external and internal reality is somehow more or less constant.

Having written this, I feel depressed by it, because it suggests that we are all missing out on happiness. We are either too young to appreciate and use our opportunities, or too old to have these opportunities. At all ages we can manage to grasp some happiness if we are lucky, but something is always in the way of complete fulfillment. There is all that happiness flying around, elusive to be sure, yet available if we could only overcome our own limitations and those of society. It is there but out of reach because when we have the vitality and freedom necessary to capture it, we are all messed up inside, too worried about who we are or where we are going. By the time we have resolved (if not solved) those problems, we lack the vitality and freedom necessary for the pursuit of this elusive item. Thus, youth may be wasted on the young, but wisdom is just as surely wasted on the old. So we go along, getting some degree of happiness but never being just the right age to get as much as we should be able to.

This may be too bleak a view, and frankly I do not really believe it. It seems clear that on average, people of various ages have some combination of internal problems, external problems, and actual opportunities that even out so that they attain about the same level of happiness. However, it is also clear that at all ages there are some who are enormously happy. These are presumably the ones who do manage to "get it all together," who overcome whatever problems they may have and grasp the opportunities that come along or make their own. The fact that some can do this means that it is possible and we are not all doomed to lives of, at best, moderate happiness. Moreover, all of the evidence is that attaining this high level of happiness is possible at all ages and the chances may even increase with age, at least up to a point.

One final comment. It may well be that asking children and adolescents how happy they are produces answers that cannot be compared to those of other ages. As we get older, our perspective changes. A little boy's delight in a terrific new toy may seem shallow and trivial to his older sister who's in love for the first time; and her parents may smile indulgently at her puppy love, thinking that a full, loving, adult relationship is a much richer source of happiness. There is no way to resolve this problem. Just as we can never know whether someone else's perception of the color red is identical to ours, we can never know whether someone else's happiness corresponds to our own. Perhaps the child is made just as happy by the new toy as the adult is by the perfect relationship. We must keep in mind the possibility that they are experiencing different levels or degrees of the same feeling, or even that the feeling is different. The one argument against this is that people of age fifty-five must have a quite clear memory of their experiences at thirty-five, and when the former say they are just as happy as people who are younger, it seems to me that the answers are probably comparable. We may not remember how we felt when we got a new toy, or even during our first romance, but most of us can remember our adult experiences pretty well and can compare, at least roughly, our happiness at various periods. Thus, our finding that reported happiness changes little with age is probably an accurate reflection of how people experience life.

8. In Sickness and in Health

"If you've got your health, you've got just about everything."

—TELEVISION COMMERCIAL

Most Americans are healthy. In our surveys, 80 percent rated their health excellent or very good, while only 6 percent rated it poor or very poor. And most people who are healthy take good health for granted. They ignore it unless and until it is absent. Naturally, older people tend to be less healthy and worry about their health more than younger ones, but the difference is smaller than you might imagine. Many people who are in poor health seem to enjoy considerable happiness, while the reverse is even more often true—a fair number of healthy people are unhappy. Thus, even though we all think of good health as an essential prerequisite to happiness, the relationship between health and actual happiness is rather weak and shows up mainly in extreme cases.

When someone is very sick, to the point of dying, it is obviously difficult for him to enjoy life in the same way as healthier people. Although there is not enough evidence to draw firm conclusions, it seems as if only at this stage—when bad health becomes associated with death or fear of death—does health make happiness difficult if not impossible. Consider the case of a young man of twenty-two. Over the past ten years his life has been about as happy as he expected it to be. But the last six months have been quite unhappy because he is sick—dying of cancer. "I had cancer surgery in August and am facing more surgery because it

120

is in fact terminal. I keep all this to myself—not even my family knows that this is terminal. I don't want anyone to know—yet, secretly, I think it would be so nice for someone to find out and pity me, comfort me. It is hard to be twenty-two and wondering and questioning why you can't be happy and why you have to die. People teach us many things but not how to cope with dying. It's scary and so lonely . . ."

Of course, how could we expect him to be happy? Not only is he dying, but he is dying alone, with no comfort from anyone because he keeps it (or thinks he keeps it) from his family. In fact, it is quite typical in cases such as this for the family to think that the patient doesn't know, while the patient thinks they don't know. Thus, each must bear the additional burden of maintaining a secret that is not a secret; and neither can talk about the situation and get some comfort from sharing it.

This is the extreme state of bad health. However, many people with bad but not fatal health problems seem to manage to be quite happy and even to obtain some additional happiness from their ability to cope with their difficulty. For example, we talked to a woman of twenty-nine who is living with someone, has an active but not very satisfying sex life, and is happy with her love life and friends. She describes herself as moderately happy and optimistic about life. She is a graduate student in psychology, thinks she is doing well in her work, happy with her growth as a person, quite sure of herself and happy with who she is. She has had a severe kidney problem since birth. It made her early years very unhappy, but now: "The physical symptoms I listed [in answer to the questionnaire] are due mainly to my kidney dysfunction. I know they are sometimes considered psychosomatic, but in my case they are a direct effect of the kidney trouble. This physical problem, which I was born with, made my childhood very difficult but I have now manged to cope with it. Naturally, it still makes many things in life very hard and interferes with lots of activities. Suffice it to say that I'm quite pleased with my ability to cope with this health problem and lead a worthwhile and happy life in spite of it or perhaps partly because of it."

Although this woman's poor health does make some things more difficult and is always a consideration in making plans, even on a day-to-day basis, she has worked out a way to live with it. Moreover, she has gained a sense of mastery from her illness which adds to her self-confidence. Of course, there is no way to know for sure whether she would have been even happier if she were perfectly healthy. But this and conversations with other people suggest that moderately bad health—not fatal disease but nevertheless serious problems—affect people in very different ways. Some people are made miserable; the bad health seems to poison their whole life and remove any chance of happiness. Others cope with the problem, incorporate it into their lives as one more thing that must be dealt with, find their happiness relatively unaffected by their bad health. Judging from the information we have, it seems that most people adapt very well to poor health as long as it is not too bad. Of those respondents in one study who said their health was moderately bad (the second worst category), 70 percent said they were at least moderately happy in general compared to 76 percent in the whole population. For these people, their poor health made only a small difference in their happiness. In contrast, of those who said they were in very poor health (the worst category) 55 percent said they were at least moderately happy in general, still a reasonably high figure but considerably less than the rest of the population.

It should come as no surprise that good health does not guarantee happiness. In one survey, over 50 percent of those who were very or moderately unhappy with their lives were in good health. Perhaps more to the point, those who were very or moderately happy were only slightly less likely than the rest of the population to be in poor health (4 percent versus 7 percent). In other words, like many other factors, good health does not produce happiness. Poor health may prevent it for some people: it is obviously easier to be happy if you are healthy, but you can have good health without happiness and vice versa. At the extreme, as described earlier, it is probably an unusual person who can be happy while suffering from certain extremely debilitating diseases or progressive illnesses that are likely to be fatal, especially if they occur when the person is young and has every right to expect to be healthy. But outside of these relatively rare cases, most varieties of poor health merely make happiness harder to attain rather than eliminating the possibility.

Health and Attitudes Toward Life

State of health does affect attitudes toward life in a variety of ways. As you might imagine, healthy people are more optimistic about their own lives and the country in general. They also feel that they have more control over what happens to them in life, both the good and the bad, and are less likely to feel that when things are going well it will not last. All of these relationships are quite weak, but they present a consistent picture of a somewhat rosier view of life. Considering these findings, it may be that health matters more than most of us realize or than the data seem to show, but that the effect of happiness is indirect. Thus, the healthy person who is optimistic about his life may attribute his happiness to his optimism, not to his health, without which he would not be optimistic. Similarly, good health may be an important source of a person's feeling of control over his life, at least control over the physical aspects which depend so greatly on having a healthy body. Asked why he is happy, this person might give credit to his sense of control over his destiny, not realizing that his good health is essential to this sense of control. Moreover, when we look at the relationship between health and happiness, the effects are small because so many other factors, such as those we just mentioned, intervene. The relationship is not direct—good health does not make us happy—but it does produce these attitudes which themselves play a large role in happiness. All of which is another way of saying what we mentioned at the beginning of the chapter: most Americans are in the fortunate position of being healthy and therefore being able to take their good health for granted.

Other People's Health

Although people's own health has only a small visible effect on their happiness, the health of loved ones seems to play a larger role. We do not have good evidence on this relationship because none of the large surveys asked questions specifically on this topic. However, the more limited, face-to-face interviews plus letters we received indicate that one of the most important causes of unhappiness is the bad health of lovers, spouses, children, and parents. Many people seem to be able to cope with their own poor health, but very few can deal effectively with having a sick child. Many people told us that they would be very happy except that someone close to them was ill.

There may be selfish reasons for the unhappiness that results from someone else's illness. There are, after all, more demands on you when you are healthy and the other person is sick. The sick need to be cared for, their meals cooked, their bedding changed. Medical expenses may strain the budget and worry the breadwinner. The sick must be entertained and made happy. People who have to care for a sick relative may feel that they have no control over their lives, that they cannot choose freely what to do each day, that they cannot even let off steam, grumble and grouse, so as not to upset the sick one. This entails guilt because you are healthy and the other is not, guilt because you must at times resent having to care for the other, guilt because you may be tempted to leave the sick person or even wish he were dead.

Take, for example, a woman of thirty, happy in a second marriage, very happy with her love life and her sex life, and reasonably satisfied with her friends and social life. She works as a clerk and is a part-time student, her husband is a policeman who earns over fifteen thousand dollars a year, and they live in a small city. In many ways, her life seems fairly good, but she considers herself very unhappy, because of a sick child. "A product of the 50's, I married at 15, had two children I was left alone to support at 17. My oldest son was born with a congenital disease, muscular dystrophy, a progressive condition which requires a great deal of care. He must be dressed, lifted from bed to chair, bathed, hair combed, teeth brushed, fed. He is totally unable to care for any of his bodily needs. Nursing is the last occupation I would have ever wanted, yet I do it daily, including turning him over every two hours during the night.

"I literally turn over my paycheck to cover help for his care so that I may work and go to school. I was 25 before I could continue my education to get a high school diploma. I now have two years of college behind me and hope to be able to continue my education.

"Death is nothing new to me, but living with it on a day to day basis is, and it's very difficult. Obviously I live with constant guilt over feeling resentful. I also love my son and have enjoyed the challenge of working with various groups to better things for handicapped children. But I have never known autonomy, independence, without the dependence of others or free choice."

When someone you love is sick you suffer both from the necessity of taking care of him and also from the sense of loss and the sympathy you feel. Several people described the terrible effect of watching a parent or, more often, a spouse die. Even when the healthy spouse is not heavily burdened with the responsibility of caring for the sick one, the experience is awful. Indeed, there is independent evidence that the loss of a spouse is one of the most difficult and upsetting experiences that people can endure. The loss of a parent, even a very elderly one, is also very upsetting. Presumably, a slow death due to illness makes both experiences even more difficult.

The illness of a spouse can cause unhappiness even if there is little love in the relationship. Someone who might leave a spouse who was healthy might be unwilling to leave one who is ill; moreover, sickness usually entails financial problems, thus putting additional pressure on everyone involved and making divorce or separation even more difficult. Many people stay with sick spouses and sick parents out of obligation, guilt, and other motives good and bad. But often the net effect is that the sick person gains little while the healthy one suffers enormously. We heard from one woman in this situation, a thirty-seyen-year-old married woman with one child. She is an executive secretary but does not earn much money. Although she is happy with her role as parent, with her success in life, her job, personal growth and health, she is very unhappy with her marriage, sex life, social life, and financial situation. Not an ideal situation, perhaps, but hardly unusual and not on the surface especially difficult or unhappy. Yet she describes herself as very unhappy because of her husband's sickness.

"I've been married over 16 years. The marriage has been unsatisfactory, my husband is withdrawn and uncommunicative and I wanted to leave him. But then, just when I was getting up the nerve, he got sick and has been disabled for a year with kidney failure. He is now waiting for a transplant which may or may not ever occur. This factor has decreased our total income by 2/3 and caused me great anxiety, worry, etc. If it were not for his illness, I would have left by midsummer this year if not earlier. Due to his bad health, he is impotent. After this occurred, I engaged in extramarital sex for the first time. Am now in love with another man. This affair has no bearing on whether I would leave my husband if he had good health—I would in any case. My troubles of the past year have totally changed my outlook on life and have forced me to grow tremendously and enlarge my tolerance of myself and others."

Although there seems to be little question that the illness or death of a loved one (or even one who is close and not loved) is usually a great source of unhappiness, many people deal well with this, just as they deal with their own poor health. For example, it is commonly believed that having a parent or sibling die when you are a child is a severe trauma that has profound effects on your life. This may be, but in our research there is no evidence that it has any direct effect on either childhood or adult happiness. In one survey, 4 percent of the people had a brother or sister die when they were children, 10 percent lost one parent, and 1 percent lost both parents. Yet we found no relationship between these events and happiness, attitudes toward life or anything else. I am certainly not suggesting that losing a parent or sibling is a minor event in a child's life—it is probably one of the most important things that can happen. But the effects are either temporary or very subtle in most cases.

Even in adulthood there are people who seem actually to gain some satisfaction from another's illness, not because they want the other to suffer (though I suppose this happens occasionally, but that is another story), but because it gives them a chance to take care of the other, to show their love, and to take on responsibilities. Just as some nurses and physicians presumably take pleasure in treating others, making them comfortable and so on, nonprofessionals can get the same kind of satisfaction from taking care of sick people who are close to them. Indeed, relationships between people may sometimes improve because of illness, as is shown by a letter from a man of thirty-eight who has been married for ten years, has two children, works as a foreman in a factory, and says that he is moderately happy with life. "I have almost no free time because before I go to work and as soon as I get home, I have to do things around the house and for my wife. She was in an accident two years ago. Her legs were badly hurt so she can't get around at all; and she also has trouble breathing because of damage to her ribs and lung. She's had lots of operations, and she is a little better, but she can't do much for herself. The kids help some, but they are too young to do much. So I do most of the housework, cook, wash my wife—it keeps me busy and tired. But the strange thing is that we get along better than we ever did. She seems to appreciate what I do for her, and I don't mind doing it. Sometimes it's a drag, but mostly it is OK and we love each other more now than before. Also, the kids took it very well and the whole family is very close."

Of course, as indicated in a letter quoted earlier, often people resent having to take care of someone who is sick. Unfortunately we do not have enough information to know which response is more common. However, it is important to realize that people have both reactions—sometimes dealing well with the situation and even benefiting from it.

Beauty and Obesity

"I would like to be myself only 35 pounds thinner . . ."

—SURVEY RESPONSE

Although most Americans do not usually have to worry about their health, we do as a society devote a tremendous amount of time, money, and energy to physical beauty. The manufacture and sale of cosmetics is a five-billion-dollar industry; there are countless health spas and diet clubs, the biggest of which, Weight Watchers, is a multimillion-dollar business. A remarkable number of people—one estimate is over 20 percent at any one time, and this is probably too low—go on diets to lose weight or to stay thin. And there is evidence that Americans place a premium on physical attractiveness. Controlled research by psychologists shows that attractiveness plays a major role in choice of friends and lovers—we all tend to prefer to associate with people who are nice looking. Given a choice between two people who are similar in other ways, we pick the more attractive one not only for dates, lovers, and spouses, but also for friends, partners in work, and just about every other social relationship. We even assume that people who are attractive have all sorts of other positive traits that have absolutely nothing to do with appearance. For example, asked to guess someone's intelligence, we tend to guess that attractive people are smarter than less attractive ones. More attractive people have been judged to have higher status in their occupations, to be better marriage partners, to be happier in their professions, more charming, more honest and so on. Foolish, perhaps, but we all tend to do it.

From all of this, you might surmise that it is a great advantage to be attractive and that it would have a substantial effect on one's life in general. Beautiful or pretty women and handsome men should lead better, easier, more successful lives. They should make friends more readily, get better jobs, and have better love lives. And surely, you would imagine, all this would make them happier. One of the surprising findings from the research on happiness is that attractiveness has very little effect. Overall, there is little or no relationship between attractiveness and sexual satisfaction—more attractive people are slightly more satisfied than less attractive people, but even here the relationship is so small as to be almost meaningless.

Versus Men

However, when we look at men and women separately, we find that physical attractiveness does matter appreciably for women though not for men. In one study, people were rated on attractiveness by a panel of other people, thus avoiding the possibility that people might overrate or underrate their own looks. Those who had been rated were, naturally, not told that they were being rated or how they fared. But they were asked how happy and satisfied they were with their lives. When the independent ratings of attractiveness were compared with the people's own ratings of their happiness, entirely different patterns emerged for the two sexes. There was no relationship between appearance and happiness for men; but women who were rated more attractive also tended to be happier.

This is a provocative finding that, of course, agrees with what women have been complaining about for years—that unlike men, women are valued more for their appearance than they should be, that they are treated according to how they look, that they are treated as sexual objects or ornaments, and so on. For some reason, how men look does not much influence their lives, whereas women are defined in part, perhaps in large part, by their physical attractiveness.

Among the letters and interviews we collected, we found many women complaining about their appearance, wanting to be better looking, listing physical appearance as one of the most important influences on their happiness. In contrast, almost no men mentioned their appearance—it simply is not one of the key factors for them.

Focus on Fat

Most often women complained about being overweight. In questionnaire after questionnaire, interview after interview, they said that being fat was preventing them from being happy and that being thin would provide happiness or at least make it possible. An eighteen-year-old woman who is 5 feet 7 inches tall and weighs 170 pounds, and who seems to be doing quite well in life said: "I would not want to be any other person. I would like to be myself only 35 pounds thinner." She says that she is moderately happy with just about everything else about her life—she has lots of friends, a good sex life, and so on. Obesity is the one thing she would like to change.

Most of those who are overweight are less happy with some related aspects of their lives than people who are not obese. A twenty-one-year-old woman who has a good, high-paying job and enjoys good health is totally dissatisfied with her sex life and her love life. She told us: "I would change lives with a friend only because the one I am thinking of is slim, and, unlike myself, not overweight. Outside of that one reason, I would not change lives with anyone as I have had an excellent education and some very good times with friends and relatives."

Another woman who complained about her weight is married and has no children. She works as a high school teacher, earns almost twenty thousand dollars, really enjoys her work, thinks she is successful at it, and is generally happy with her personal growth and development. She is also reasonably satisfied with her marriage, social life, love life, and finances, but is dissatisfied with her sex life, in which she suffers from various problems including difficulty in reaching orgasm. She believes in God and an afterlife, has had feelings of harmony with the universe, and believes very strongly that her life has meaning and direction. She also feels that she has control over both the good and bad things in her life. All in all, quite a self-confident person who seems to be doing well in all phases of her life except perhaps sex and who, in fact, considers herself moderately happy. What does she want? Brains and beauty, mostly the latter. "I wish I were smarter but, more important, I wish I had a size nine figure. The reason for this is that I feel fat and ugly [she is 5 feet 4½ inches and weighs 162 pounds]. I don't have any will power when it comes to food."

There are various reasons why obese people are less happy. In the first place, the world probably does treat overweight people, especially women, less well. They are less popular with the opposite sex, less likely to be picked for good jobs, and are discriminated against in all sorts of subtle ways. However, the unrealistic, symbolic reasons may be more important. In our society obesity is considered unattractive and also, in some sense, a sign of poor self-control. Both attitudes are presumably shared by those who happen to be overweight themselves. Thus, they consider themselves unattractive and this must lower their own self-esteem. They think less of themselves, think that they are in some way inferior people, and this affects their happiness directly. It may also affect it indirectly because if you think less of yourself, you tend to behave less freely, less spontaneously, and less confidently; and this makes you actually less fun to be with, thus producing what may be called a self-fulfilling prophecy: you think you are inferior, you act as if you are, and soon you are.

The issue of self-control is also of great importance. The woman quoted above feels that she has control over the good and bad things that happen to her in life, but most obese people feel that they lack control over themselves. Other people can control their eating; fat people cannot—or at least they think they can't. As we shall discuss in a later chapter, a sense of control plays a role in happiness. To the extent that you feel out of control, you tend to be unhappy, and obese people, lacking a certain kind of control, should accordingly be less happy.

One important consideration regarding obesity is that one's attitude toward it may be much more important than the actual poundage. There is growing evidence that some people are naturally heavier than others, that their "normal" weight may be considerably greater than others of the same height and build. In other words, some people, because of some internal body mechanism, are naturally "overweight" compared to the average person. However, this may be the best weight for them—they are not obese, they are just heavier. If they simply accepted the fact that this is the way they are built (just as we accept the fact that some people have longer arms or thicker necks than others) they would be fine. They would be just as healthy as anyone else. The problem is that in our society it is considered "bad" to be heavy, and so they try to lose weight. This means that they are constantly dieting, eating less than they want and perhaps need, and, in fact, harming their health. Moreover, they are depriving themselves of food, suffering with some awful diet, and, unfortunately, generally having only limited success because they are fighting their natural weight. The evidence suggests that it is the people who try to lose weight who are most unhappy and show the most negative side effects. If someone told you that your arms were too short and you should try to make then longer, and if you undertook some program to lengthen them, you would be miserable when it turned out that the program was painful and your arms stayed the same length. Thus, current research indicates that within limits (I am not talking here about the extremely obese, just those who are 15 or 20 percent over average and have almost always been) extra weight has few if any physical ill effects and it is dieting and worrying about obesity that makes people both unhealthy and unhappy. In other words, just as with physical attractiveness in general, it is the person's own attitude that is most important.

The research on health and attractiveness provides the fascinating result that only three aspects of physical well-being seem to have substantial, consistent effects on happiness: 1. very serious illness or physical disability, such that your health is very poor and you are either dying, in great pain, or almost totally unable to take care of yourself; 2. the same kind of condition affecting a loved one or one with whom your life is bound up; 3. a woman's obesity. Less serious health problems may have some effect on happiness, but it is very small; physical attractiveness and obesity count little or nothing for men; and even physical attractiveness, excluding obesity, has only a small effect for women.

9. Income and Education

"If I were a rich man . . ."

—FIDDLER ON THE ROOF

People work for money, make decisions based on it, envy those who have more of it, have contempt for those who have less of it, marry or divorce for it, and constantly hope to have more of it than they do. Given three wishes, a great many people would include wealth as one of them. Throughout our research on happiness, we found people who said that if only they had more money, they would be happy. "Let's face it," wrote a sixty-two-year-old man a few years from retirement, "money is the name of the game. When you don't have enough of it to do the things you like to do, there is no law against dreaming and wishing. If I had enough money, when I retire I could have woman who is thirty-one years old, married, has one child, and a wonderful time going places, fishing and enjoying life." Another, working as a computer programmer making fifteen thousand dollars a year, told us: "The need to earn money has had too great an influence on the direction my life has taken and on how I spend my time and energy. Money would give me the freedom to reject roles that do not suit me . . ." And a twenty-three-year-old unmarried man who works as an electronics technician says: "I wish I were a person who isn't so restricted in his activities as a result of his dependence on money. Frankly, I feel that I spend too much time trying to earn a living and not enough time living." People want money for freedom, for independence, for specific needs or interests, for power, for status. Many of them think that money would solve their problems and bring happiness. But does money buy happiness? The proverb says no. The answer from our research is yes and no: money is not very important to happiness if you have even a moderate amount of it; but if you don't have enough to live on, it matters a great deal.

Poor but Happy? Don't Count on It

In 1975 the Gallup polling organization conducted a survey in countries all over the non-Communist world and included questions on happiness. In each country people were asked how happy they were and were given three choices: very happy, fairly happy, and not too happy. In all, 8,787 people in North America,

Latin America, Western Europe, Asia, Africa, the Middle East, and Austrialia answered this simple question.

There was one major, overwhelming finding: people in poor countries say they are much less happy than do people in rich countries. The wealthiest countries, those with the highest average income per person, report a very high rate of happiness as measured by this question. Almost everyone in Western Europe, Japan, Australia, and North America (excluding Mexico) says he or she is either very happy or fairly happy. The figures ran as high as 95 percent in Canada and Sweden, with the United States, West Germany, and the other richest countries only a point or two behind. These figures probably overestimate the number of people who are actually quite happy—compared to the other surveys done on happiness, the question was worded in such a way that people tended to overstate their actual feelings of happiness. Thus, the specific numbers should be taken with a grain of salt. For example, from more careful studies we know that it is not true that 95 percent of the people in the United States are happy. But for purposes of comparing one country to another, the Gallup figures are useful, and for any purpose it is impressive that so many rate themselves happy in these rich countries.

As we descend the income scale by country, the populace rates itself somewhat less happy. Countries such as Italy and England, whose economies were in a severe depression when the poll was taken; and Spain and Portugal, which have always been less wealthy, produce happiness ratings of between 60 and 80 percent. There is not a perfect relationship between income and happiness, but generally the richer the country, the greater the happiness. However, the big difference occurs with the really poor countries—places where most of the people are lucky to live at a subsistence level, where people go without food for days and constantly wonder where their next meal will come from, where shelter is terrible and disease rampant. Others have provided more vivid descriptions of life at this impoverished level than I ever could. The point is that in these countries most of the people have a much lower standard of living than even the poorest Americans. Indeed, many of these countries have an average yearly income of less than two hundred dollars, some well below that; and social services are often nonexistent.

When we consider these countries, the rates of happiness are desperately low. In India only 20 percent of the people say that they are even fairly happy; in Pakistan, only 22 percent; in Colombia, only 24 percent. That is, almost 80 percent say they are not too happy, the lowest choice offered. Apparently, when you are trying simply to stay alive, when your primary and constant concern is satisfaction of the basic needs for yourself and your family, notions of pleasure, satisfaction, contentment, and excitement have little meaning. When asked about happiness people in this state may not even understand what it is supposed to mean; but assuming they understand it the way we do, very few of them seem to experience it.

So, to begin with, let us be clear. At the extreme low end, income makes a huge difference in happiness. The very poor are generally not happy. Fanciful notions of the simple person with no money, little food or shelter, working terribly hard, suffering hardships but managing to go through life with a smile are just that—fanciful. There may be some people who, by some mysterious process, some fantastic inner strength or marvel of personality (or neurotic self-delusion), can live in poverty and be happy. But by and large this does not occur. People with no money may be pure, hardworking, honest, moral, sensitive, religious, and fine, generous souls, but they are rarely happy. Their rewards do not come in this life.

The American Poor

Within the United States, Canada, and most of the countries of Western Europe, although there is a wide range of incomes, the contrasts are much less great than between these countries and the poor countries of the world. An income under fifty-five hundred dollars a year for a family of four is considered below the poverty level in the United States. Unfortunately, there are over twenty million people with incomes this low or lower. Moreover, more people than most of us would like to believe actually live in deep poverty, going without decent food or shelter much of the time. There is no denying that poverty does exist here, despite any inroads that the Great Society may have made on the problem. Without in any sense glossing over this disheartening and terrible situation, it is still fair to say that this is a rich society where, compared to other countries, relatively few live without at least the essentials of life.

The importance of this for our purposes is that once some minimal income is attained, the amount of money you have matters little in terms of bringing happiness. Above the poverty level, the relationship between income and happiness is remarkably small. The effect of income within our country shows up almost entirely at the very bottom of the income scale. The very poor and the poor say that they are less happy than everyone else. When we survey people with a family income of less than five thousand dollars (and in some studies with less than ten thousand dollars), fewer of them say they are very happy or moderately happy and more of them say they are very unhappy than people with higher incomes. However, even among people with these low incomes, a high percentage seem to find life pretty good: in most studies, considerably more than half of the low income groups still describe themselves as either very happy or moderately happy, while fewer than 5 percent say they are very unhappy. These figures vary only a little from study to study. In other words, within our society, even those with the lowest incomes seem to find considerable happiness in life and few of them are miserable.

Money Buys Less Today—Even Less Happiness

The influence of income on happiness seems to be diminishing. Research by Angus Campbell and his associates found that twenty years ago there was a much greater difference between the happiness of the rich and the poor than there is now. The reason for the change is not that poor Americans are much happier than they used to be; rather, it is that the rich are generally less happy. This is a fascinating finding that we do not fully understand. Presumably it has something to do with social changes that have taken place over the past two decades. Later we shall discuss some of the possible reasons in more detail, but one obvious one deserves to be mentioned now. During the 1960's and '70's there seems to have been some reconsideration of what is called the work ethic—the belief that a person's goal in life is to get a good job, work hard, make money, and get ahead. Most of us continue to do, or try to do these things, but we have begun to question whether they are the *real* goal, whether they are the ends in themselves. In particular, upper-middle-class, college-educated people went through a period of considerable disillusionment (connected with Vietnam, drugs, politics, loss of faith in government and in religion). Although most of these people continued to go through the system and today, more than ever, are applying to medical and law schools, seeking the successful life, they do it with less confidence than before. They do not expect life to be good just because they have gotten into medical school and will become rich doctors. Indeed, according to their reports, life is not good just because it's prosperous.

Thus, we can speculate that while many people at the upper ends of the income scale were becoming disillusioned by the work ethic, most of those at the lower end continued to hold to their original goals, especially that of making enough money to live comfortably. This means that the rich and well-to-do are less sure just what they want from life, and less sure what to do with their money, than the relatively poor. Accordingly, the poor are just about as happy now as they used to be, while the rich are less so. I am not by any means suggesting that we should therefore feel sorry for the rich folks—there is no question that they are better off than the poor. Yet it becomes increasingly clear that money does not buy them happiness; indeed, that it buys them less happiness than it used to.

The Rich Are Not So Different from You and Me

To return to the effects of income on happiness, the most important finding of the research is that income makes little or no difference except for the lowest groups. Those with incomes of ten thousand dollars say they are just as happy as those with incomes over thirty thousand dollars. In some surveys there are slight differences favoring the richer groups, but generally just about the same percentage of people in each group report themselves very happy or moderately happy, and also the same percentages say they are very unhappy. The rich are not more likely to be happy than those with moderate incomes; the middle class is not more likely to be unhappy than those with lower incomes. As long as the family had enough money to manage, which seems to be about ten thousand dollars these days, their reported happiness is at most slightly related to how much money they have. For the majority of Americans, money, whatever else it does, does not bring happiness.

On the other hand, there is no indication that money produces unhappiness. Just as there is a myth about people being poor but happy, there seems to be some feeling that having a great deal of money somehow interferes with happiness. The rich are too concerned with material goods, their life style is not conducive to good personal relationships, rich mothers leave their children with governesses and go off to work or to the hairdresser, rich people have no morals, and so on. They may have lots of money, but their lives are not as good as those of people with more modest incomes. None of the surveys showed this. As we would expect, people with higher incomes were happier with their financial position and their jobs than those with lower incomes. But the rich were just as happy with the social aspects of their lives as were the middle class. Those with incomes over thirty thousand dollars were at or near the top of the scale in terms of satisfaction with sex, with marriage, with their spouse's happiness, and with having children. They were not more likely to have extramarital affairs than were poor people, nor were they any more likely to be divorced. Indeed, on all of these measures,, the only substantial difference among income groups was that the very poorest groups were less happy with almost everything while all other groups were about the same. In other words, although money does not bring happiness, it does not appear to introduce extra problems. People with high incomes are just as likely, and perhaps a little more likely, to be happy with each separate part of their life as those with less. Financial situation matters much less than most of us would have thought. It is only slightly related to general happiness; but it still seems, on balance, better to have more than less money even in terms of finding happiness.

Money and Parkinson's Law

Anyone who has watched his or her income grow has probably experienced a variation of Parkinson's Law that I like to call the Law of Expanding Expenditures. The original law was that the amount of work expands to fill the time available to do it: if you give someone a week to complete a job, he may be able to do it; if you give him a month to do the same job, he will take a month; and if you give him six months, he will take that long. Likewise, our expenditures seem to expand to use up the money we have. If you make five thousand dollars, you may just manage to live within that amount; if you then make ten thousand dollars, you also just get by; and even if you make thirty-five thousand dollars, at the end of the year, you have nothing left. Whatever income you have, eventually you get used to spending just about all of it—or if you are the saving type, you save the same percentage of thirty-five thousand dollars as you did of ten thousand.

As a student, I lived on what now seems no money at all, but I lived in a style which seemed perfectly fine. My apartment seemed then (and in retrospect still seems) like a lovely apartment, though it was not luxurious. I ate out as often as I thought I wanted to. I do not remember denying myself anything because of money, though I suppose I did. When I got a job, my income more than doubled. My rent also just about doubled. I ate out about as often as before, but the restaurants were a little more expensive. I do not remember denying myself anything because of money, though I suppose I did. As my income has grown since then, I have spent more on apartments and on restaurants and on other things, but it has always seemed to be just about the same amount of money and bought just about the same things. The major change is that I have spent more on everything, and I consider buying more expensive items. None of this has had an appreciable effect on my life or on my feelings of happiness or satisfaction. I imagine that if I earned five times as much, the same would be true—at least it would once I got used to the extra money. This is not to say that I would turn down a raise—quite the contrary. But after a while everything would settle down, the extra money would no longer be "extra," and my life would be the same as before.

Many people have reported similar feelings in our surveys and in personal interviews. A very thoughtful, sensitive woman who recently became enormously successful in her career and earned many times as much as she had previously, remarked that she got great satisfaction out of her *success*, but the *money* did not necessarily make her happier. She explains that both the success and the money make her feel better when she is in a good mood anyway, but worse when she is feeling bad. And, in any case, she quickly got used to drinking better wine.

This may not be a typical reaction, but it is clear

that the happiest people are not necessarily rich. This may be because we change our goals and they keep moving away from us. We used to want a Chevrolet, now we want two Pontiacs. Or perhaps it is because the possessions don't matter much as long as we have enough to live on—they are luxuries, unnecessary extras that might be fun to have for a moment but give no lasting satisfaction.

Higher Goals

Another possibility is that once basic needs are satisfied, we turn to higher, more complex goals that in many ways are more difficult to satisfy. As long as you are poor enough so that you must worry about necessities, you can concentrate on everyday needs that are relatively easy to deal with. You worry about getting enough food and shelter; then, with a little more money, you worry about getting nicer clothes, good schooling for children, or whatever you happen to find important. But the focus of your life is on these basic elements that may be hard to find without money but are not complex psychologically. However, once you do have a reasonable income and the basics are provided, you have to think about such imponderables as growth, self-expression, success, and achievement. And worrying about these things takes more out of you, the solutions are harder and chancier and even more difficult to recognize once found. So with little money, the basics make you happy or lack of them make you unhappy; with more money, the more complex, higher needs do the same. In both cases, your level of happiness is about the same because however much money you have (up to a point) new needs replace the old ones. Of course, poor people must also worry about "higher" goals to some extent, but the emphasis changes with more money.

Whatever the reason, it is clear that in the United States, except for the lowest income group, money is not a major factor in happiness. The very poor everywhere are less happy than the rest of the world. But once you have enough to live on in reasonable comfort, your income makes little difference to your general happiness.

Education

"Where ignorance is bliss, 'Tis folly to be wise."
                              —THOMAS GRAY

If money can't quite buy happiness, perhaps education can. We have all been taught that education is the key to the good life, the ticket that allows us to climb the social and economic ladder, the element necessary to get good jobs—those that pay well and are interesting and rewarding. Education does lead to a higher income and, generally, a broader range of job opportunities. Only with an education are you at all free to enter many of the "desirable" fields of work—teaching, medicine, law, engineering, etc. And many other fields are effectively if not formally closed to the uneducated because employers prefer to hire those with college or graduate degrees. Although, as we have seen, money is only slightly related to happiness, education would seem to give a person so wide a range of options that the effect on happiness should be greater. Moreover, the educated man or woman is schooled in a wide variety of ways that allow him or her to appreciate sophisticated pleasures. He or she is not only more likely to be able to afford fine wines, trips to Europe, an extensive library, seats at the opera, and perhaps even esoteric sexual delights; he or she is also more likely to know about such things and how to enjoy them to the fullest. At least, this is what we are often told.

Education and Income

There is no question that level of education is closely related to the income you will earn. For example, consider white males in the United States. Of those with twelve years of education or less, that is, who have no college, almost 50 percent earn less than ten thousand dollars a year and just under 85 percent earn less than fifteen thousand. Those with some college, even if they did not graduate, are much better off financially. Sixty percent earn over ten thousand dollars and a full quarter earn over fifteen thousand. And with a college degree or more, income increases dramatically. Over 70 percent earn over ten thousand dollars with almost half earning over fifteen thousand. In other words, the chance of having an income over fifteen thousand dollars is almost three times as high if you have a college degree than if you had not entered college, and almost twice as high than if you had not finished college. True, 17 percent of those with no college do manage to earn over fifteen thousand dollars and 12 percent of those with a college degree earn less than six thousand. Education does not guarantee a high income; lack of education does not make it impossible. But the more education you have, the better your chance of earning a lot of money. The figures for women and nonwhites show comparable effects of education, though unfortunately the percentages earning high incomes are lower.

Education and General Happiness

It should come as no surprise that many studies have shown a small but consistent relationship between education and happiness. People with more education describe themselves as happier. In one of our studies, over a third of those with at least college degrees said they were very happy, while less than a quarter of those with less education were very happy. Similarily, at the other end of the scale, almost twice as many people without a college degree were very or moderately unhappy as were those with the degree.

However, the relationship between education and happiness is not a simple correlation between years of schooling and amount of happiness. The big difference seems to be between those with and those without a college degree. There is at most a small difference between those who never went to college and those who went but did not finish; there is not even much difference in terms of happiness between high school graduates and high school dropouts. At the other end of the educational ladder, there is little or no difference in reported happiness between people with a college degree and those who have graduate training of some kind. Indeed, in at least one study, those who have a graduate degree are less happy than those with only a bachelor's; in another study, the two groups rate themselves the same. Thus, the key point in education in our country at the moment (at least in relation to happiness) is the college degree.

In this respect the results of the research coincide superficially with the widespread belief that a BA or its equivalent is the passport to success and, implicitly, happiness. However, this is a substantial overstatement, because, in fact, none of the differences among educational levels is very large. True, in the study cited above, those with a college degree were happier than those without one in terms of the percentage that were very happy. But the difference in percentages was not great (less than 10 percent) and if we combine those who described themselves as very happy with those who were moderately happy, the educational levels become quite similar (the biggest difference is then only 5 percent favoring the college educated). Many people with little education are happy; many with years and years and degrees and degrees are miserable. Education helps, but by itself it is a relatively minor factor in happiness.

Education, Income, and Happiness

We have seen that, somewhat surprisingly, neither income nor education seems to play a major role in happiness. Once some minimal level of income is surpassed (above the poverty level or a little higher) more money is not related to more happiness; and the effect of education is small at all points. Yet on the face of it one would think that both of these basic social factors would make a great deal of difference in one's happiness—not guaranteeing happiness, of course, but making it more attainable. Especially when advanced education is combined with high income, as it often is, we should expect the result to be greater happiness.

One explanation for the lack of effect of education and income is that highly educated people expect so much from life that they are easily disappointed. If they get what they want, the argument goes, it gives them little pleasure or excitement because they knew all along that it was coming. If they get less than they expected, even if this is a great deal more than most people get, they are disappointed and upset. In contrast, those with relatively little education expect less. If they get little, they are not disappointed; if they get a lot, they are pleasantly surprised. In other words, as I suggested earlier, happiness depends in part on the relationship between expectations and outcomes, with the best situation being to get more than you expect.

A major study of the quality of life in the United States provides some support for this idea. It considered the relationship among education, income, and general well-being, which we can think of as similar to happiness (though it may not be identical). Overall, both education and income tended to be associated with higher levels of well-being—just as we have seen. But the fascinating result was that people with college degrees and high incomes were actually less happy than those with the same income and no degree. In other words, the happiest groups were those with little education who earned a lot; while the highly educated who earned a lot were not so well off psychologically.

These results can be explained in terms of expectations. After twenty years in school you expect and perhaps even think you deserve to make lots of money. If you then make twenty-five thousand dollars a year it is no big deal. Worse, if you expected to make lots of money, twenty-five thousand dollars may seem disappointing—less than you expected. Whereas someone with no college degree might consider this a sizable income and a sign of success, the highly educated person has higher sights and is let down by the same income that delights the other.

A second, more complex explanation is that money can never be a source of much satisfaction for the highly educated. Instead once some adequate income is achieved (and this might be a fairly high amount but still fairly easy to attain), the person looks elsewhere for satisfaction and happiness. He turns to feelings of achievement and creativity, a place in life, making contributions to the world, being recognized in his field as opposed to just making a good salary, interpersonal relations, personal growth, and so on. These abstract goals are harder to achieve and more ephemeral than just lots of cash. According to this argument, while the less-educated person is having fun with a big income, his more-educated counterpart is worrying about "higher" things, more complicated, less accessible goals, and is actually less happy. This is an elitist notion—and there is little evidence to support it. But it may be true, at least for some, and I offer it as something to consider in addition to the simpler explanation in terms of expectations versus achievements.

We can find support for either of those theories in the case of a twenty-five-year-old single man with a college degree. Until recently he had an excellent job that paid well, lots of responsibility and freedom. He has many friends, leads an active sex life with which he is very satisfied, considers himself above average in attractiveness. He is in perfect health, does not use drugs, drinks little, and has no physical or psychological symptoms. He is happy with all of the social aspects of life (though he is not currently in love). On the surface, he seems to have just about everything one would need for happiness with the exception of a long-term romantic relationship. Yet he describes himself as moderately unhappy and has, in fact, just decided to return to school because he thinks perhaps that is the answer.

"I look back over the past four years since I graduated from college and what I've done, and it's generally been guided along the pursuit of happiness. I've had many things that many people regardless of age have envied me for, much traveling, a job of good pay and responsibility, personality and physical looks. After college I thought I was all set—the world was mine. And I did get most of what I wanted, but it didn't add up to much. All these things haven't pleased me as much as I thought they would or as much as they seem to please other people. I don't know why, but it all was nothing once I got it. So now I find myself back in school trying out one more thing to see if it will work."

He is a perfect example of the man who has everything but is still unhappy. His solution, to get more education, may work for him, but clearly up to now all his education has not done the trick. It may even have interfered with his happiness, perhaps by handing him the world on a silver platter, perhaps by leading him to expect too much. He adds that ". . . the one thing I want, that I would envy someone for would be real achievements. I want to feel a little different from the average person, to make a mark on the world, I have lots of education and a good job, but I haven't done anything worthwhile." While it may be admirable to have a desire to achieve something important, it can also be a source of frustration and unhappiness, since so few ever accomplish anything outstanding. And perhaps college gives some people the idea that they should stand out, make a mark, when in fact they are unlikely to. This can make all the real achievements in their lives seem hollow because they are not big enough to live up to this vision.

Education and Specific Areas of Life

Perhaps by looking at various aspects of life we can begin to understand more fully just how education affects us. When we consider these areas, we see that education has substantial effects on some but no effects on others. Moreover, the relationship with education varies appreciably for the different areas.

As we would expect, education does have substantial effects on people's happiness concerning their financial situation, their feelings that they are getting recognition and achieving success, and with their job. All of these are closely associated with one's occupation, and education provides more occupational opportunities. As with general happiness, the big split is between those with a college degree and those without one; graduate training does not increase happiness, nor does a lack of any college reduce it compared to those with some college. But if you have a college degree you tend to be more satisfied wih your economic situation, your job, and with recognition and success.

It should be noted that education also and quite understandably is related to whether a married woman works or devotes herself entirely to taking care of the home. But here the only real difference is produced by graduate training. Surprisingly, those with college degrees are only a little more likely to have jobs outside the home than those with only high school educations. But if a woman has an advanced degree, she is much more likely to have some kind of employment outside the home. This additional training is not especially related to other kinds of satisfaction, but it does affect employment.

In contrast to these employment-related feelings, education is not at all related to various social aspects of life. Highly educated people and those with little or no education do not differ in terms of their satisfaction with their health, friends, love, sex lives, and marriage. These central aspects of life, which seem to be more important for happiness than anything else, are unaffected by education. This is certainly part of the reason that education has only a low overall relationship to general happiness. It may make you happier with your work and your finances, but they are only a small part of the recipe for happiness; the social part, which is more important, is unaffected. Moreover, women with *little* education tend to be happier with family life in general and their role as parents in particular. This is not a strong effect. Highly educated women also enjoy their children and their families, but there is a slight tendency for women with less education to enjoy them more. And this may to some extent balance the greater happiness the educated women find in their jobs.

Education and Attitudes Toward Life

Education is related to general attitudes toward life. There is a consistent tendency for those with more education to have more positive attitudes about the world—not necessarily about other people, but about life as a whole. When asked whether they have confidence in their own guiding values, those with a college degree or more say they are considerably more confident then those with less education. The more educated are also more optimistic about their own lives—this is especially true of women—though less optimistic about the country as a whole. In other words, they seem to feel more solidly rooted, to know what they want and what they believe, than the less educated, and this translates into optimism.

Many psychologists and psychiatrists have argued that it is very important for people to feel that they have control over their own lives. Modern society often robs us of this feeling because everything is so big, fast-moving, and impersonal that things happen to us for reasons we cannot understand. We are distressed and unnerved by being constantly exposed to situations and forces beyond our control. I shall discuss this argument in a later chapter; for the moment, the point is that education appears to lessen these feelings of loss of control. One question on several surveys was: "When things are going well for you, do you often feel that they can't last?" People with more education were less likely to agree. Another question asked about how much control people thought they had over the good things in their lives; again, educated people thought they had more control.

All of this makes good sense. Education does not, of course, guarantee control over one's life, but in many cases it helps. It gives you more options, more choices.

Rather than having to accept what the world provides in terms of a job, you can choose. You can select what field to study in the first place, and then usually have a wider choice of jobs later than someone with less education. Although we often hear it said that a liberal arts education doesn't prepare a person for a career, there is no question that most employers prefer college-educated people for a great many different jobs. In addition to this realistic aspect of the benefits of education, people with a college degree may know more about how society and government function. This sometimes makes them cynical, but it may nevertheless give them some sense of control. Even though they may think that everyone in government is a crook and that big business and big government do not care at all about individuals, the college graduate's knowledge of the system probably makes him or her believe that he or she is less likely to be taken advantage of than someone with little education. And it is probably correct that college-educated people are more likely to avoid being cheated, to complain about mistreatment, and to try to fight what they consider mistreatment than those with less education. All of this is, naturally, highly variable from person to person. College people get cheated constantly, and many people with no education are a lot sharper and less likely to be taken advantage of than their college counterparts. But there is some tendency for education to be a defense, or at least to seem like one.

Overall, both money and education have small relationships with general happiness. In both cases, there seems to be some point above which more money or education does not matter much. With money, this cut-off point is very low—only the very poor are clearly less happy on average than everyone else; once above this level, income has only a slight relationship with general happiness. With education, the critical point is the college degree. At this time in our society, those who have completed college are on average somewhat happier than those who have not. Neither factor should be considered crucial to happiness; neither seems to count as much as social relationships or various attitudes toward life. But each contributes a little. Also remember that according to one major study, if you have a college education, a substantial income makes you less happy than if you do not have that much education. Presumably, only a much greater income will satisfy a college graduate, so that in some instances education can produce disappointment rather than happiness.

One final point is that although education does not guarantee happiness, it does not generally (with the exception just noted) do the opposite. Some people seem to think that education ruins us by making us too sophisticated, or raising our expectations too high, or making us spoiled. Glorifying the "noble savage," they sometimes write as if the uneducated have the best chance at happiness. This, along with the notion that the poor are happier, must be visions held only by the highly educated, rich, and cynical. It is a patronizing view and those who hold it would never change places with the blissfully ignorant and poor whose praises they sing. None of the evidence supports this romantic notion. Money and education may have only small relationships with general happiness, but what there are favor the rich and educated. It is true that some people with little education and large salaries are happier than those with more education who make the same income, but we must not forget that far fewer uneducated people make these good incomes.

10. Work

Most people spend more time working than doing anything else. To a great extent we define ourselves and others define us by the kind of work we do. Our occupations determine where we live, who we have as friends, the style and pace of our lives, our conversation, and generally where we are in the social order. Accordingly, it would seem that being satisfied with one's job, feeling that it is worthwhile, enjoyable, and that we are good at it, should be one of the most important sources of happiness.

Not only do we spend a large amount of time at work, we also usually stick with the same kind of work all our lives. Of course, many people change jobs—they receive promotions or move from one company to another or from one position to another similar one—but very few change careers entirely, from bricklayer to musician or from musician to accountant. If at some point in your life you decide that you do not like the line of work you are in, you are legally free to change without asking anyone's leave. But making such a change is extremely difficult and very few dare to try it. It is probably easier to change mates than to change careers, even though marriage involves a legal commitment and requires legal proceedings to terminate it. Although accurate statistics are hard to get, one estimate is that two people in a hundred voluntarily change careers (as opposed to being fired—stockbrokers who

153

drive cabs for a while are not counted). In contrast, 50 percent of marriages end in divorce. This may mean that people are happier with their jobs than with their mates, but I doubt it. Rather it must be due to the enormous difficulty of changing careers. Some people do manage to switch from medicine to architecture, factory worker to small businessman, painting to corporate law. But very few do because such a change involves a dramatic reorganization of their lives. People who want to switch fields often must get special training, return to school, undergo financial sacrifice (at least for a time), make new friends and associates, and so on. They also have to face the strain and risk of starting over. A forty-year-old businessman who would like to be a lawyer may be willing to go through law school competing with the younger, more energetic students; may be able to get into the school and through it; and may have enough money to manage it. But such a person must also be willing to start at the bottom once school is over. This is not easy and so it is hardly surprising that few try it. Changing spouses is also difficult, and involves some of the same problems, but either they are seen as less severe or the motivation to get out of the marriage is stronger than to change jobs. In any case, it is clear that the choice of career is much more binding and much harder to get out of than choice of spouse. And this fact too should make our jobs especially important to happiness.

Job and Happiness

Sure enough, almost everyone *says* that his or her job or main occupation is very important to happiness. When we ask people this, they rate work as high as anything else—over 90 percent consider job either very or moderately important to their happiness. And dissatisfaction with a job is a very common complaint, with many people saying that if only they could get a better job (any job, if they are unemployed), or be promoted, or change something about their job, they would be happy.

Consider the case of a forty-nine-year-old married man with some graduate education. He is only neutral toward his marriage, his two children, his love and sex lives. Overall, he says he is neither happy nor unhappy, but he suffers from a variety of symptoms including ulcers, high blood pressure, insomnia, and feelings of worthlessness and loneliness. He drinks too much and knows he does. Clearly, quite a set of difficulties, which he blames on his job. He says: "I would be much happier if only I could have a different job. I would like to be a professional person, an optometrist, attorney, or medical doctor. Or maybe I could own my own business—it would be good to run a restaurant or a home improvement center. The reason I want this is so that I would be able to see and feel the immediate results in my endeavors. Also, and most important, I could be in control of my own work enviroment and not dependent on individuals in the corporate structure." Yet he has what most people would consider an excellent job as a business executive in which he earns well over fifty thousand dollars a year.

This man—whose job seems, on the face of it, to be quite good, but whose social and family life is unrewarding—nevertheless focuses on his job as the problem with his life. He does not complain about his income (though he is not totally happy with it); he does not emphasize difficulties with success or recognition (though he is not totally happy with either). The reasons he gives for his unhappiness are that he has to fight the corporate structure or at least be controlled by it and that he does not see the immediate effects of what he does. (I suppose from his point of view it is too bad that he blames his job for all his problems, since changing jobs is much harder than changing just about anything else.)

Complaints about one's job are relatively rare among people like this who are older and already established. Older people tend to be happier with their jobs. Many more complaints are voiced by younger people who are just starting or trying to start a career. They wish they were more advanced, that they had their supervisor's job, more seniority, or more security. They also seem to wish that they were more sure about what kind of job they wanted to spend their lives in. But generally, what they want is to be immersed in a satisfying job. One twenty-seven year-old man who is studying biology suffers from a host of symptoms—insomnia, constant worry, trouble concentrating, irrational fears, crying spells, and feelings of worthlessness. He is dissatisfied with his sex life, unhappy with his financial position, and feels that most of the things that happen to him are not under his control. What does he want from life at the moment? To get his degree so that "I will be able to do what I am trained for and what I desire to do." To him the degree seems almost to be a magic wand that will make everything right. He does not ask for special success or a particularly good job, just the chance to work at what he wants. This is a fairly common plea, unsurprisingly, given the high unemployment in the United States during the past decade, and especially the plight of people trained in academic fields, where the number of teaching and research jobs has dropped sharply.

For most people a job plays a much broader role than merely providing income. As I shall discuss later, satisfaction with a particular job depends in part on the money you make, but this is not the most important factor; nor is it the major reason most people want to work. For example, a twenty-three-year-old woman who is about to get married, has a college degree, and is happy with every social aspect of her life—friends, love, sex, marriage—does not have a job at the moment. She seems to be a well-adjusted, happy person who knows what she wants, and right now she wants a job. Even through her fiancé can support her adequately, she says: "I would be happier if I found a paying job (I am presently volunteering) in my field. This challenge would enable me to have a greater sense of personal worth, independence and freedom." For her and for millions or others, the job is needed, both for money and especially because it will give her a feeling of doing something worthwhile. Although volunteering is somewhat rewarding, for her and for many others, it is not equivalent to a regular job.

There are, of course, many people who are unemployed and do not have any money. The woman described above wanted to work, but did not have to for economic reasons. Work is very important to her, even though she has the luxury of not needing it. For those without money a job, any job, takes on even greater significance. With the unemployment rate running 6 percent—a great deal higher among younger people and startlingly high among nonwhite teenagers—there are millions of people who are looking for a job and not finding one. Most of these, especially the younger ones, do not have any money. For them a job means getting off welfare, raising their standard of living, and—what is perhaps most crucial—having some sense that they are true members of society.

Consider the case of a twenty-nine-year-old black man who is married, has two children, and until recently was working as a packer in a publishing company. Eleven months ago he was laid off because business was slow. Since then he has been living on unemployment insurance and looking for work. Although he is moderately happy with most aspects of his life, and very happy with his marriage, sex and love life, and with his children, he describes himself as very unhappy primarily because of all that being unemployed entails. "I never much liked the job when I had it because there wasn't much to it except putting stuff in boxes and packing them up. But the people were nice and it was OK being there. Now I wish I had that job or anything. We are living on unemployment which won't last long and we can't make do now. The kids haven't had new clothes except borrowed, we don't go out or do anything, and don't eat so well. All I do all day is hang around. I stay home and the wife goes crazy; or I sit around with some other people on the block and there isn't anything to do. When I had the job I felt like I was somebody—not much, but something. Now it's all a waste of time."

And a twenty-three-year-old woman who completed two years of college and went out to find a job. She got one as a secretary but was let go after three months because the job was abolished. She is unmarried and lives with her parents. Her situation may not be as desperate as that of the man just described, but it isn't good. "I keep looking for some job—I'd take anything—but there are so many looking that I don't seem to have a chance. They always ask about experience. I don't have any so those who do get the jobs. But how can I get experience if I don't get a job? So I sit around at home all day or wander around the city with nothing to do. No money to buy anything; no one around because most of the people I know are working. I feel as if my life hasn't really gotten started. I am ready to start work, to get going, and there isn't anything there for me."

In the case of unemployed people, it is difficult to know if the job is more important for the income it would produce or the sense of worth it would provide, though both are important. Among employed people, however, there is evidence that money is not the whole story.

In one survey we asked the question: "If you suddenly inherited a large fortune, would you continue in your present work (including student)?" The idea was to find out how many people really like their jobs, and also how many were clear either that they wanted to do something else or would prefer not to work at all. We found that over 60 percent of the people were certain that they would remain in their present work and another 10 percent were unsure. Only 30 percent would either switch or quit entirely. While this is a substantial number, it indicates that most people are not working only to earn a living. Even if they were rich, most of them would continue doing what they are doing now. It may well be that economic pressures played some role in their choice of occupation and perhaps in how hard they work; but in our society, there still seems to be strong feeling that it is good to work and that a job is a source of gratification and satisfaction aside from the money it produces.

Whatever the particular sources of satisfaction in work (we will discuss this more later), it is clear that those who are happy with their jobs are happier in general. In Chapter 9 we saw that money alone plays a small role in general happiness. Satisfaction with one's job, however, is one of the most important factors, surpassed only by love and marriage, and equaled by various social and personal growth considerations. In one study, 70 percent of those who were happy with their job were happy with life in general, whereas only 14 percent of those who were unhappy with their job were happy in general. It is not impossible to be happy without being satisfied with your job, but it is much harder.

Marital Status, Sex, and Job Importance

The role that job satisfaction plays in general happiness depends to some extent on one's marital status and sex. For both single men and single women, occupation is at or just below the top of the list of factors affecting happiness. Job is more closely related to general happiness than anything except life and love. Most single adults are also relatively young. They are starting in their careers and are involved in all of the crucial decisions that entails. They have to pick a career, figure out how to get a position in it, how to advance in it, and so on. They also have to decide whether they like it once they do begin, and what special line they want to take within the general field. There is, as they say, lots of action and lots of turmoil. It is not surprising that their jobs are so important in their lives at this time. Moreover, many single people are not in a long-term love relationship. Thus, marriage and family life, which will eventually become exceedingly important for most people's happiness, have not yet entered their lives. They are deeply concerned about finding some person to love, but marriage with all it entails is in the future.

In contrast, married people of both sexes find that job (including homemaker) is less important to happiness than it is for single people. For married men it ranks fourth on the list, below personal growth, marriage, love; for married women, it ranks even farther down, seventh on the list, behind love, marriage, partner's happiness, sex, personal growth, and recognition, and equal with friends and social life. (Note that it is not the single people for whom sex is more important than job, but married women, a surprising finding.)

The shift in emphasis from job to married life is easily understandable. You are now married, usually have a family, and all of this distracts you somewhat from your job, takes its place to some extent, and provides another source of happiness or unhappiness that for most people is at least as compelling and urgent. The interesting finding is the shift for women when they are married, which presumably is due to the fact that many married women do not have paying jobs or consider their work of less consequence than their families. This is not to say that they are dissatisfied with what they are doing (which may include housework) but merely that their occupation matters less than the interpersonal, marriage, and family parts of their lives. In other words, a single man or woman or a married man tends to be unhappy if he or she is unhappy with a job; and happy if he or she is happy with a job; this relationship between job satisfaction and happiness is much weaker for a married woman.

Job Satisfaction

We know that satisfaction with one's job is closely related to general happiness, and that this relationship is stronger for single people than for married people. This leaves one crucial question unanswered: what produces job satisfaction? Because this is such an important question, and I suppose in part because so many big companies are concerned with it, there have probably been more studies on this problem than almost any other in psychology or sociology. Although all of this research has not given us final, definitive answers, it does tell us a great deal about what people look for in jobs and what gives them satisfaction.

In the first place, it is reassuring to know that between 60 percent and 70 percent of the people are moderately or very happy with their jobs, while perhaps as many as 20 percent are quite unhappy. Considering everything—that some people are just starting out, that others have not been able to get a job in the field they want, that others are disappointed in their degree of success and so on—this is an impressive level of satisfaction. It does not mean that most people are delighted with their jobs or that they think their jobs perfect; but it does seem that most people like what they are doing well enough to rate it fairly high. And, as we mentioned earlier, most of them would stay in their job even if they did not have to for economic reasons.

There are two sides to the question of what brings job satisfaction—characteristics of the work itself, and characteristics of the people doing it. To start with the former, many different studies involved asking people what the most important aspects of their jobs were in terms of giving them satisfaction. Although the results differ slightly depending on who is answering and when, five characteristics of the job stand out as most important for most people: the interest level of the work, chance for advancement, financial considerations, security, and whether the work seems worthwhile. Various other factors that you might think would be crucial, such as how friendly the other workers are, the surroundings, the boss, how good you are at what you are doing, and so on, are rarely if ever mentioned. Although they may rate very high for some, most people consider them much less important then the big five listed above.

We have already noted that income is not as important an aspect of work satisfaction as one might expect. It always ranks quite high, but is rarely the major factor in choosing a job or in finding satisfaction with one. Overall, higher income is associated with more job satisfaction, but the major difference is between those with the lowest incomes and all others. Moreover, there is good evidence that the actual amount you make is less important than how your income compares to others who are at about your level. For example, in one study, supervisors who were earning over twelve thousand dollars were found to be considerably happier than company presidents who were earning under forty-nine thousand dollars. Even though the presidents were earning almost four times as much as the supervisors, the presidents felt underpaid (presumably because other company presidents were earning much more than they), while the supervisors felt fine because their salaries were high for supervisors. You are not dissatisfied with your salary or with your job because some movie actress or rock star or the chairman of the board of directors of General Motors is earning a huge income—their salaries are irrelevant to yours. But you do feel dissatisfied if the person down the hall, who is doing just about what you are, is earning even a little more than you, because it means you are being underpaid. Similarly, if you are the one who is earning a little more, you feel good even though somewhere in the world other people are earning a lot more than you. What seems to matter is a comparison of your income with the income of those whom you consider approximately equal to you in terms of responsibilities, duties, and so on.

Security, chance for advancement, and whether the work is worthwhile seem to be obvious factors in job satisfaction. More and more, security has become the major demand of union workers, superseding salary as the primary concern. And in all jobs, people rate security as very important. Similarly, it is hardly surprising that people like to have some chance for promotion and that they like their job to seem worthwhile. All of these factors are fairly straightforward, though what people consider worthwhile must vary greatly.

However, the fascinating question is what makes a job interesting and enjoyable. This is the first factor mentioned by most people, the one that, understandably, is most closely related to overall job satisfaction. But saying that an interesting job is satisfying tells us almost nothing, because we still want to know what makes it interesting. It is almost like saying a satisfying book is one that is interesting and enjoyable—sure, so now tell me what makes it interesting and enjoyable. Unfortunately, this isn't so easy when it comes to either books or jobs. There is a movement among some companies to make their jobs more satisfying by what is called "job enrichment." This involves increasing worker responsibility, autonomy, and the skill required; as well as giving more recognition for work done, introducing new tools, procedures, and equipment, giving workers greater voice in decisions, and generally trying to upgrade the job in terms of the amount and level of work required. Many companies report that this has increased job satisfaction considerably, so perhaps we should consider all of these factors in job interest and enjoyment. Quite simply, it suggests that the more responsibility and skill involved, the more enjoyable the job will be.

This seems plausible. Executive positions seem more interesting than those lower down; supervisors have more interesting jobs than assembly-line workers; or so it might appear. Yet several studies have cast doubt on this simple notion. This research rated a wide variety of jobs in terms of how demanding they were—how much autonomy, responsibility, variety, and skill they required. Then they asked people in each position how satisfied they were with their work. Surprisingly, they found no relationship between the level of the job, in terms of how much it demanded, and satisfaction. It turned out that some people preferred the demanding jobs, but others did not. Some people were more satisfied when they were required to make decisions and take responsibility, but other people were more satisfied when very little was asked of them except to do the work.

It seems clear that people differ greatly in what they want from a job and how it fits into their lives. Some consider a job central, they define themselves in terms of the job ("I am a steelworker"), while others think of the job as something they do for eight hours a day and then their real life starts ("I am a man who works in a steel mill"). For the former, demanding jobs bring more satisfaction; for the latter, anything that requires them to devote more energy to the job makes it less satisfying because all they want is to get through the eight hours as quickly and painlessly as possible. Thus, it is difficult to say what makes an enjoyable job and make it apply to all people. The enrichment program described above will make a job more enjoyable for those who really care about the job in the first place while it may be a nuisance for the others. We can say that for a large percentage of the population a more demanding, more responsible job is more enjoyable while another large percentage of the population will be happy with exactly the opposite. Although this may sound as if we know nothing, actually it enables us to define two kinds of people and perhaps then to offer different jobs to each. That way maybe we can match people with the kind of job that is most likely to satisfy them.

Aside from the specific characteristics of jobs that bring satisfaction, we do know that the status of the position is strongly related to job satisfaction. Professionals and managers (executives, store owners, etc.) are much more likely to say that they are very satisfied with their job than any other group. Next come clerical workers and sales people, then skilled and semi-skilled workers, and finally unskilled workers. The difference between these various positions is, of course, caused by many factors. The higher on that scale you fall the more money you make (usually—teachers do not always make more money than sanitation workers), the more flexible your hours, the more status you have in the community, and so on. It is difficult to know what the key factor or factors are that bring greater satisfaction, but there is no question that generally higher status jobs bring more of it. This is reinforced by one study that asked people in various fields whether they would choose the same work again if they had the chance. Almost all mathematicians said yes (91 percent), most lawyers (83 percent), and journalists (82 percent), but only half of the printers (52 percent).

Among skilled car workers only 41 percent said they would choose the same field, and among unskilled car workers only about a fifth (21 percent) would. Clearly, higher status fields include many more satisfied workers.

In this respect, it is interesting to compare college and noncollege people in terms of job satisfaction. Daniel Yankelovich noted in a recent article that a great many noncollege young people are upset and frustrated because they feel that all of the "fulfilling" jobs are closed to them. Without the college degree, most of the jobs that our society considers high status and interesting are out of reach. And the young person without the college degree feels left out right at the beginning, with no chance to find true satisfaction in work. While this attitude is certainly understandable, the actual difference in job satisfaction among college and noncollege workers is not very large. Naturally, because as we just noted high status jobs tend to be more satisfying, college workers are generally more satisfied. But the difference is quite small overall. The fascinating result is that on almost every characteristic of the job, the college and noncollege groups rate their jobs approximately equal. They are equally satisfied or dissatisfied with the financial aspects of the job, with security, the enjoyment level, with fellow workers, and with the degree of self-determination provided. The one big difference is in terms of how worthwhile they consider the work, and on this one factor, the college-educated group rates their job much higher. In one sense, this agrees with Yankelovich's point that the "fulfilling" jobs are out of reach—but only if we assume that fulfilling means worthwhile. I suspect that the young people think that these jobs are also better in many other ways, and in that respect they appear to be overstating the differences.

Time on the Job

In describing the conditions necessary for people to be happy in their work, John Ruskin included the idea that "they must not do too much of it." We also know that "All work and no play makes Jack a dull boy," and presumably that holds for Jane being a dull girl if she works too hard. Yet, we all must know some people who work endless hours and love their work. They may be dull outside, but they find satisfaction in working long hours. Just how does time spent working relate to satisfaction?

In the first place, there is considerable evidence that people like flexible hours, especially when they provide more time for leisure activities. Many studies on four-day weeks, work-when-you-want schedules, and other kinds of systems that are more flexible than the standard five-day week find that flexibility leads to greater satisfaction. One of the key characteristics of a job that people almost always ask about right away is the number of holidays. This is not necessarily because the people do not like to work, but because they do like to have vacations. So, in this sense, the proverbs are right—people like more time off and more flexible hours.

However, the most interesting question concerns the relationship between how much a person works (assuming some freedom in hours) and satisfaction with both work and life in general.

One of our happiness surveys asked some questions that are relevant. We asked how much time was spent in various activities—on the job, with one's spouse or partner, with children, in leisure activities and so on. Generally, we found that how people divide their time is unrelated to happiness and to almost anything else. The only relationships we found are obvious. For example, the more time spent with your spouse, the happier you are with your marriage, love, sex, and spouse's happiness. This is hardly surprising, and may be due to the fact that if you are happy with your spouse, you spend more time with him or her. Yet we did not even find this kind of obvious relationship when it came to time spent at work. Those who work longer hours are not happier with their jobs (nor are they less happy); they are not happier with their spouse, marriage, or family, nor are they less happy. Indeed, the only substantial relationships with time spent at work are with income (longer hours, higher income) and education (longer hours, more education). We also asked people whether, if they suddenly inherited a great fortune, they would continue in their current line of work. As discussed earlier, most people said they would. However, there was no relationshp between answers to this question and how much time spent at work.

This pattern of results (or nonresults) suggests strongly that there are many different reasons why people spend a lot of time working. Some probably love their work; others hate their wives or husbands and work in order to get out of the house; others have no outside interests and so have nothing else to do; others work mainly in order to earn money or get famous; and still others are forced to work long hours by the kind of job. Thus, some work long hours because they are "workaholics" who practically have to force themselves to stop working. Some of these reasons for working so much—hating one's spouse, having no other interests, and "workaholism"—probably mean that the person does not especially like the job and, more important, is probably not very happy with other aspects of life or life in general. Other reasons—really liking the job, having a fascinating job that requires long hours, perhaps even a drive for success—may mean that the person does enjoy work and may also enjoy life in general. And still others such as being forced to work long hours, or needing the money may be irrelevant to job satisfaction and happiness. The point is that we can make no general statements about the relationship between time spent working and happiness, because there are different reasons for working long hours and they have different implications.

What is the relationship between a particular occupation and general happiness? This is different from asking how happy people are with their jobs themselves. It is the more central question of how people in various jobs rate in terms of overall happiness with life. There are two answers: first, it does seem that some kinds of jobs are associated with more happiness than others; but second, there is overlap, people in every kind of job are happy and unhappy. As with everything else, job alone neither guarantees nor eliminates the happiness.

Overall, those in the professions and service fields are happier than those in lower status jobs, especially those that tend to involve repetitive tasks. Thus, at the bottom of the happiness ladder are people in clerical jobs (considerably below all the others). Then come bookkeepers, keypunch operators (despite the supposed glamour of computer work), secretaries and stenographers, and blue-collar workers (factory, etc.) At the upper end of the happiness scale are clergymen, psychologists, and those who describe themselves as entertainers. One could argue that all of these fields involve doing something for others, perhaps even brightening their day, though the approaches and the work itself are certainly different. The next group in terms of happiness includes architects and engineers, college professors in general, nurses, social workers, and business managers. I can see no common thread running through these jobs. Some of them involve helping people; some, creativity; some, intellectual pursuits; and some, straight business. In any case, this group of occupations includes people who describe themselves as moderately happy—less happy than the clergy, etc., but more so than the clerical and secretarial group.

One of the enigmas of this survey (which is the only one that has detailed information on the happiness level of people with particular jobs) is that lawyers and, even more so, doctors rated themselves as relatively unhappy. There are not a great many representatives of either—or of any occupation—so the results may be unreliable. But assuming they are accurate, why should these two professional groups consider themselves so unhappy? Doctors were less happy than nurses; lawyers less happy than engineers. Yet they seem to have everything one would want in a field; at least they seem this way to the tens of thousands of students who apply each year to medical and law schools. What could be wrong?

Doctors have by far the highest average income of any group. True, money does not buy happiness, but no one has ever suggested that it didn't help a little. Most doctors and lawyers are self-employed or are partners in a joint practice, so they have autonomy, self-determination, flexible hours, and, usually, nice working conditions. Surely, most of them think their work is worthwhile, delivering babies, curing illnesses, saving lives (even cleaning up a little acne is worth doing); as is defending the accused, prosecuting the guilty, fighting for civil rights, arranging a divorce (though perhaps not making more money for a corporation). But even if some doctors consider acne a waste of time and fixing up a nose even worse, and even if some lawyers deplore corporate practice, overall these two are considered "service" fields that provide useful and necessary service to other people. They would seem to have everything going for them, and we know that professionals, including doctors and lawers, are generally more satisfied with their jobs than anyone else. Yet they are unhappy in general. Puzzling.

Perhaps people in these fields are so involved with their work that they do not get a chance to enjoy life. Even in these days when house calls are a distant memory, doctors do seem to work long and tedious hours (some do, anyway—others seem to take four days off a week). The same is true of lawyers. They may find satisfaction in the work, but are so exhausted from it that they do not find happiness in general.

All of this is, of course, highly speculative. Generally, as I said earlier, those who are satisfied by their work are also happier. Why this is not true of doctors and lawyers, and whether our particular doctors and lawyers are representative, is uncertain.

We have seen that people in higher status jobs tend

to be more satisfied, and that job satisfaction is an important ingredient in general happiness. But we have also seen that different people respond very differently to various aspects of their work, some liking and thriving on responsibility and high demand, others disliking it. Moreover, although college-educated people are more satisfied with their work than noncollege, the difference is small. And although higher incomes tend to be associated with greater job satisfaction, the difference there is small also. Thus, I think the lesson from all of this is that having work that you enjoy and find satisfying is very important to happiness, but the particular type of work, the specific job, is much less important than the person's response to it. People can be satisfied in virtually any kind of job, and dissatisfied in any kind. Getting a particular job does not guarantee satisfaction, nor does it guarantee that you will be dissatisfied. Different people find entirely different kinds of work satisfying, and I suppose there are people who find satisfaction in almost anything they do while there are others who are always dissatisfied with their work. As we have always been told, having a satisfying job tends to bring happiness; but there are no easy, simple rules for finding such work.

11. Town and Country

"Fields and trees teach me nothing, but the people in a city do."

— SOCRATES

"God made the country, and man made the town."

— WILLIAM COWPER

"The country is lyric,—the town dramatic. When mingled, they make the most perfect musical drama."

— HENRY WADSWORTH LONGFELLOW

Americans move constantly. The latest figures show that the average person moves every four years. There is a seemingly incessant flow from towns and farms to cities, from small cities to large ones, from large cities to huge ones, and then, in reverse, from the biggest cities outward to the suburbs. People move for all sorts of reasons—to look for work, because they are transferred to another job, to go to college, to be with someone they love, because they are dissatisfied with where they are, because they hope somewhere else will be better. There is an undercurrent of feeling that whatever is wrong with life in one place will be taken care of someplace else, that what is missing here will be present there. Many hopes may ride on changing where you live—but all the evidence shows that the grass is no greener on the other side of the fence.

Happiness and Type of Community

A big city like New York is an entirely different environment from a farm, a small town, or a small city, Indeed, there are those who claim that the sheer size of New York makes it different from everywhere else in America. The life you lead, your day-to-day experiences, the people you meet, your activities, job, means of transportation, social life, food—everything depends in part on where you live, and life in one kind of community is quite different from life in any other kind. Yet people's level of happiness does not differ from one place to another. Many studies indicate that people who live in rural areas, towns, small cities, large cities, huge cities, and suburbs are all just about equally happy. Even though the rate of poverty varies considerably from one type of cummunity to another (it is much higher, for example, in cities and rural areas than in suburbs) and poverty is associated with unhappiness, there is still virtually no difference between suburbs and other kinds of communities. Survey after survey shows that the happiness level is the same every place. There are minor differences in the various surveys. One found that rural people and those who live in small cities (25,000–250,000) rated themselves slightly happier than urban- and suburban-ites. But another survey, this one more representative of the whole population, found that rural people considered themselves the least happy, and those who live in the largest cities (over 3 million) rated themselves the most happy. In all cases, the differences are minuscule and since they are not consistent, I think is is accurate to say that the type of community has no overall effect on happiness.

One interesting result is that although they are equally happy now, people in rural areas expect to be less happy in the future than urban people. Whereas a great many of the latter expect to be happier ten years from now than they are today, only a bare majority of rural people do. This may reflect the actual state of affairs in our country—rural life is relatively static and unchanging, and to the extent that it is changing, it has been declining economically and socially. The move has historically been from rural areas to towns and cities, and people who live on farms and other rural locaions must be aware of this. Thus, although they are happy now, they may be less hopeful about their future happiness. In contrast, cities have always been places of opportunity. No matter how bad things are today, there are seemingly limitless possibilities and the city dweller looks to these to improve his or her life. This does not by any means ensure that they will, but the hope is there. Despite their problems, city people are not resigned to their state, and look to the future for greater happiness.

There are two quite different explanations for why community is not related to general happiness. The first possibility is that the type of community simply doesn't matter very much. The characteristics of your community may affect how you spend your days, but they do not have much impact on how you feel about yourself, on whether you can make friends, on how you get along with people, on your capacity to love and be loved, on your interest in and capacity for sexual relationships, on your acceptance of yourself. These elements—which we know do affect happiness—are carried around inside you, are part of your personality and character, so that they are with you wherever you happen to live. The community provides a background, an environment within which these other factors operate; but the background has little effect on happiness.

The second explanation is that every type of community has advantages and disadvantages and they more or less balance each other out. Small towns may be quiet, friendly, easygoing, and calm; but they lack excitement, vitality, diversity, and various kinds of opportunities that are present in big cities. For some individuals the attributes of a small town are perfect and they will be happier there than in any other type of place; for other people, a small town would be just the wrong place to live in order to maximize their happiness. And the same is true of any particular kind of community. Some are good for some people; some good for others. No type of community is, in general, good for more people than any other kind. According to this viewpoint, communities do affect happiness, but the effect depends on what is good for the individual. Each person's goal should be to decide whether he is a "city" person, a "country" person, a "suburb" person, or whatever. Overall, since some people choose wisely and some poorly, and since those who live in each kind of community are just about as likely to have chosen well, people are equally happy in every kind of community.

Harmful Cities?

Seventy percent of the American population lives in or immediately around cities. Only 30 percent live in the cities themselves, and most of those who live in the surrounding suburbs depend on the city for employment, shopping, cultural events, and so on. Despite this concentration in and around cities, there seems to be a strong antiurban bias in the United States. Many people dislike and fear cities, and there is a general assumption that cities are harmful to people. Yes, we say, people live in and near cities, but not because they want to, only because they are forced to by the structure of society. If only society could be reorganized, we would do away with cities and live where God and Nature intended us to—on our own private farms surrounded by acres of trees and lakes. Cities are unnatural, people were not "meant" to live in them, and they hurt us in all sorts of ways.

This idyllic view of the country and satanic view of the city are wrong—wrong psychologically, wrong sociologically, and wrong historically. Cities are different from the country and have many problems, but cities are just as natural places to live as towns or country areas, they are just as healthful for their inhabitants. Living in a city does not have bad effects on our social, physical, or mental health, nor does it make us less happy with life in general.

There is by now quite a bit of evidence that cities are not harmful to your health. Indeed, because better medical care is usually available in urban centers, city people are, if anything, in better shape than country people. There are certain areas of the world, the Caucasus in Russia for example, where rural people seem to live almost forever and to be perfectly healthy throughout; but aside from these odd places, location has little to do with health. In the United States, Canada, and other industrialized countries, there are only minor variations from one location to another. Certainly, there is no evidence that living in one type of community—city versus town, suburb versus rural, large city versus small city, or whatever—shortens life-spans or damages health.

The same is true of nonphysical conditions. The rates of mental illness, both serious and minor, are virtually identical in all kinds of communities. You might think that the fast pace of urban life would lead to nervous disorders and mental breakdowns. It doesn't. Maybe it should, but people are marvelously adaptable—they get used to almost anything and even get to like it. The fast pace doesn't bother them—or if it does, it bothers them no more than boredom bothers dwellers in small towns, no more than commuting bothers suburbanites. Life is full of stress, but it is full of stress no matter where a person lives.

Though all the statistics support the belief that cities do not have higher rates of neurosis or psychosis, we all can "see" that the statistics are wrong. When you walk in a big city like New York or Chicago, you see crazy people everywhere. Every subway in New York has some maniac singing at the top of his voice; on every bus rides a madwoman talking to herself. You walk downtown in Manhattan and there is a man with drumsticks sitting in the middle of a crowded street with cars whizzing by while he plays; someone else is drawing meaningless pictures on a wall and maintaining a continuous conversation with an invisible friend. Everywhere you look, someone is acting crazy. You don't see this in small towns or suburbs. How can we believe that cities don't make people crazy?

The answer is in three parts. First, there is no reason to believe that the crazy people we see in the city were made that way by living in the city. To some extent, it's the other way around: people who are already disturbed move into cities from elsewhere. This is understandable. One characteristic of most cities is their acceptance of diversity. It has always been true that deviants of all kinds—political radicals, homosexuals, racial minority groups, and so on—find life easier in cities. They are less conspicuous and more likely to be tolerated in cities than in towns or suburbs. This does not mean that they are embraced by the majority or treated fairly. But every outcast—psychological, political, religious—shares the spotlight with many other kinds. Moreover, the long liberal tradition in most cities favors acceptance or at least tolerance of people who are "different," whether they be immigrants who speak no English or crazies who speak to ghosts. So, the first explanation is that cities attract deviants and some of them act in ways that may seem eccentric or even mad.

Second, following directly from the first, because cities are more tolerant, people are more likely to act crazy in public. If someone talked to himself in public in a suburb, he would soon be locked up or told to move on. In New York, he is ignored as long as he doesn't bother anyone too much. In West Boondock, crazy Uncle Elmer is kept indoors so he won't bother the neighbors; in Chicago, he is allowed out and probably leads a better life. Homosexuality, though not a mental disorder, provides an apt analogy. Because of the greater tolerance in big cities, the gay closet opened mostly in New York and San Francisco, not in little towns or suburbs. Some straight people may dislike open displays of homosexuality, but they are surely better for the homosexual. As with mental disturbance, there is no evidence that the rate of homosexuality is any higher in cities than elsewhere, but gays move to cities so they can lead their lives more freely; and because they can be more open, they are more likely to be seen.

Third, the population density is very high in cities, so within any small area, you are more likely to find people representing every conceivable type and with every conceivable characteristic. In a two-block walk down Fifth Avenue on a sunny summer day, you will pass thousands of people, and you can see some of everything. If you want to find a 6-foot-5, red-haired man wearing a toga, money beads, and chanting to himself, or a five-foot woman dressed in a business suit leading five Saint Bernard dogs on leashes, you will find them in a big city because you see so many more people in a given stretch of time. And if you look for crazy behavior, you will find that too—not necessarily because there is more of it, but because you see more people.

Cities Are Natural

We sometimes have the idea that cities are a recent innovation in the history of humankind. We have an image of "natural" man and woman living in the forest in families or small tribes, surrounded by thousands of acres of open territory inhabited only by wild animals. If man's natural state is rural and uncrowded, it follows that the natural state is better and the densely packed city is bad for us.

Both the assumption and the conclusion are unwarranted. It is simply not true that cities are a new phenomenon introduced by the industrial revolution or by modern civilization. The earliest city is at least eight thousand years old, and there are probably many older than that we haven't discovered. Moreover, people have always lived together in fairly large groups and under very high density. The earliest *Homo sapiens* lived in crowded caves; so did his predecessor, Cro-Magnon man. It is hard to believe, but these caves were often more crowded than today's tenements. Crowding was necessary for survival. A small group had much less chance of dealing with nature, animals, and other problems than did a larger group. As far as we know, people lived close together in settlements from the beginning.

Living surrounded by other people is not "unnatural." On the contrary, living alone on a farm might be called "unnatural" since in the "old days" no one could possibly survive doing that. It is only in relatively recent times that it has been possible for people to live by themselves. Man is a gregarious animal, not a solitary one; it is both necessary and natural for us to live with each other. René Dubos, the eminent biologist, suggested once that there may be a genetic tendency for humans to be gregarious—that it is in our genes because it was good for survival and loners died out.

Even if cities were brand new (and of course, the huge metropolis is a relatively recent development, one that was unthinkable before the industrial revolution made it possible for food to be moved quickly to town), that does not necessarily mean they are bad for us. The "old ways" are not always better; new ways not always bad. Indoor toilets and washing machines are new but most of us enjoy them and we don't seem to suffer from them. More basically, pure water, sanitation, and fast transportation are of relatively recent vintage and we benefit from them. Socially, privacy is almost a modern innovatio —the cave dwellers had no doors on their bedrooms—and now most people demand it and consider a lack of privacy for such things as sex and elimination unnatural. A lack of privacy probably was not harmful in the past and would not be now once we got used to it; but by the same token, there is no reason to believe that privacy is bad even though it is new.

It's a simple point, but those who talk in terms of our biological heritage often miss it. The antiquity of a behavior does not mean it was good for us; the novelty of another practice does not mean it is bad for us. Thus, even if cities were new (which they are not) that would not imply that they are bad. The argument that the only natural and healthy state is out in the country is false on both counts.

Apartment Living and High-Rise Housing

Although cities may not be unnatural or unhealthy, many people feel that it is not good for us to live in apartments, especially if they are high above the street. It is true that most Americans want to live in a house some day. Owning one's home is part of the American dream, and with the dream comes a feeling that a house is a more natural, nicer dwelling than an apartment, and that the bigger and taller the apartment house, the worse it is. Yet the evidence shows that type of housing has little or no effect on friendliness, health, or happiness.

There is no question that some high-rise buildings have been disasters. Some low-cost government housing has been poorly designed, poorly maintained, ill cared for by those living in it, infested with crime, vermin, and filth of every kind. In one case in St. Louis, things got so bad that the building was deliberately dynamited by the city because there did not seem to be any way to save it. Yes, high-rise housing can be bad.

But most high-rise housing is just as successful as other kinds of housing, and bad housing can be of any kind—the old tenements, only a few stories high, provided the miserable housing so vividly portrayed in the photographs of Jacob Riis. It is the quality of housing, not its height, that makes for happiness and satisfaction—and the quality of housing is influenced less by architects than by poverty, racial discrimination, unemployment, and so on. The rich East Siders in New York live in tall apartment houses having the highest population density in America, but they seem to prefer high-rises and, in fact, higher floors are more expensive to rent because they are considered more desirable. Tell these people that it is unnatural to live so high above the ground and they will tell you about their wonderful views and lack of street noise.

Various studies have compared people who lived in high rises, low rises, and private homes. Naturally, some people prefer one type to another, but regardless of preferences, where they live did not have much effect. Sociologists who have studied this in detail have concluded that type of building has no appreciable effect on happiness or anything else important.

Regions

While it may not matter how large your community is or how high above the ground you live, there are some differences in the happiness of those who live in different regions of the country. Each section has a certain reputation, and some of them, especially the West Coast and Southwest, are reputed to be lands of milk and honey, where people are carefree and happy. Although the differences are small, it turns out that, for once, popular conceptions are just about right. People in the Southwest, Northwest, and on the West Coast say they are happier than those who live anywhere else. The East and South are next, and the North Central area—the Midwest and Great Lakes regions— seem to be the least happy.

Although these results are in line with national stereotypes, it would be a mistake to make too much of them. The differences are tiny and may well depend on religious, ethnic, and economic differences rather than the influence of the place itself. There is evidence that suggests that the sunny climate of California and the Southwest is not the major factor, or at least that good climate is not necessary for happiness. People from Canada (wherever they live in Canada) rate themselves happier than those from anywhere else on the continent. Whatever the advantages of Canadian life are, a balmy climate is certainly not one of them.

Living Where You Want

So far we have been looking at aggregate figures. When we narrow our sights to focus on individuals, a different picture emerges. For individuals, happiness does depend in part on living where one would like to live. If you do not like your community or your type of community, you are much less likely to be happy than if you do. A city dweller who longs to live in the country will be less happy than others who live in cities and like cities. Similarly, màny people who live in rural areas would rather live in the city; and these people are less happy than other rural dwellers who like country life. It happens that the percentage of people in each kind of community who like their community is virtually identical—which is why the aggregate figures show no difference in general happiness. But dissatisfaction with one's community is strongly associated with unhappiness.

This makes good sense. Anthing displeasing should interfere with a person's happiness, and type of community is no exception. But it is important to realize that the effects are quite strong; satisfaction with one's community is an important, perhaps even essential factor in happiness.

We can only speculate why type of community should make such a big difference. Each kind of community has advantages and disadvantages. Anyone can make up his own list of them. But there is no question that where you live has a big effect on how you live—the pace of life, the kinds of worries you have, the activities on which you spend time, the ease of doing various things, the kind of people you meet, and on and on. It's easier, for example, to play golf in the suburbs than in the cities, to walk in the country in a rural area than in a town, to go to the theater in a city than anywhere else. So, at least in terms of day-to-day living, type of community plays a big role.

Now, each person has certain likes and dislikes, needs, pet peeves, and pet projects. A passionate stamp collector can pursue his hobby anywhere, but a passionate gardener needs land, a passionate concertgoer needs a good symphony orchestra (found only in cities), and a ballet lover will be unhappy unless he lives in or near New York. The negative side of life matters, too. A person who loves gardening but hates open spaces will be a poor candidate for life in the country; better he or she should live in town and cultivate houseplants. Someone afraid of crowds and noise would be better to pursue his interest in music with a radio and stereo set than by going to a concert hall. Thus the happy city dweller is probably someone who loves a high level of stimulation, who is nuts about theater and ballet and museums, who craves fancy foods, who likes being around lots of other people, *and* who is not much bothered by noise, dirt, waiting in lines, fighting through traffic, fear of crime, and a frantic pace of life. In contrast, someone who likes a peaceful existence, loves being close to nature, wants to grow roses and vegetables, feels best when surrounded by people he knows, *and* does not especially need the things the city person does, *or* is especially bothered by noise, filth, and crime will almost certainly be happier in a small town or rural area. Someone who falls in between, who needs the things the city offers but can't stand some of the bad features of the city, and who also needs some of the things the country offers, may be happiest in the suburbs. Each of us will be happiest in one type of community, but since we all have different needs, there are no overall effects of community on happiness.

12. *Childhood and Adolescence*

"When I was a child, I spake as a child, I understood as a child, I thought as a child; but when I became a man, I put away childish things."
—I CORINTHIANS 13:11.

Perhaps some of the secrets concerning happiness are in our personal histories. Psychologists, especially Freud and his followers, have assumed that what happens early in life profoundly affects the kind of adult one becomes. In Freudian theory, neurosis and more serious mental disorders are due mainly to problems and conflicts from childhood. Another theorist, Harry Stack Sullivan, placed the blame for some conditions at a later period, late childhood and adolescence, during which social interactions and friendships are of great importance. Whichever school one favors—even if one believes in the effect of learning throughout life—it seems plausible that experiences during childhood and adolescence should have some lasting effects on a person's mind and hence on his happiness.

In particular, early life should determine to some extent how well a person adjusts to the difficulties of adulthood, how well he gets along with others, how he deals with sexuality, and so on—all of them influential, as we have seen, on adult happiness. A tragic childhood should make it very difficult to become a normal, happy, healthy adult; a difficult, conflicted childhood should make happy adulthood harder to achieve than would a happy, carefree youth. We might think, too, that some people acquire the knack of enjoying life, by which I mean only that they develop a personality that makes the most of things and does not dwell on cares and worries. If some people do have this talent, surely childhood experiences would play a role. Where else could it come from?

All this is plausible, but, as we shall see, there is little evidence to support any of it. There are some demonstrable relationships between early experiences and adult happiness, and other adult characteristics, but they tend to be weak. Our data is, frankly, sketchy; only a few studies have collected any information at all and the information in them is based on people's recollections of what happened and how they felt many years ago, which may be unreliable. We simply do not have data good enough to justify firm conclusions, and certainly are in no position to reject otherwise sensible, plausible ideas. Nevertheless, the information we do have argues that the key to happiness is not to be found in childhood. I had expected otherwise, but am not disappointed. If it is true that childhood makes less difference than we used to think, that means people are not irretrievably damaged at any stage of their lives. They can have awful childhoods and adolescences and still grow up to be happy, healthy people. This is surely a heartening result.

General Description of Childhood

It will help to begin with an overall picture of how adults in one survey remember their childhoods. Two thirds of them say they were very or moderately happy as children (about the same as adults)—not bad even though almost 20 percent said they were very unhappy (a much higher number than adults). Going along with this are the symptoms they experienced as children (under thirteen). Seven percent had asthma, 10 percent frequent headaches, and 13 percent wet the bed beyond the usual age. A somewhat surprising 17 percent had imaginary playmates, fantasy characters, animals or people who seem to take the place of friends and whom children often believe in quite firmly, at least in some sense. About a third of the children remember being bullied and made fun of—probably fewer than actually did experience this at one time or another because older children always tend to bully younger ones occasionally. And, perhaps most important, fully a third say that they often felt guilty as children.

Everyone assumes that our relationship with our parents is a crucial factor in childhood. Our sample of people report that about a quarter of them (23 percent) came from homes in which their parents were divorced or separated. A majority (56 percent) remember the relationship between their parents (when they were together) as being very good or pretty good; a quarter say it was stable but cold; and almost a fifth (19 percent) that it was cold and conflicted. Not a very good picture of the parents when over 40 percent of the people recall mostly coldness between them. Of course, children can be wrong in the first place or remember inaccurately. Nevertheless, it is a rather chilling vision.

The relationship between each parent and child seems somewhat better. However, there is a dramatic difference between mother and father in their relationship to the child. Over 70 percent of the people say that their mother was warm and supportive to them, with only 3 percent saying she was cool and rejecting. In contrast, Dad is remembered as warm and supportive by only half the people, with 7 percent thinking he was cool and rejecting. The low end is not so bad, but the fact that only half thought their father warm is impressive. Again, memories may be faulty. More likely, the result has to do with patterns of child rearing in this country, how busy fathers are with work, how free they feel to express emotions, and so on.

Relationship to Adulthood

How happy people were as children is, of course, related to all sorts of other memories of childhood. Those who say they were unhappy also report various other complaints (being bullied or underweight, having nightmares, and so on) and also that their relationships with their parents were poor. However, childhood happiness has little relationship with anything in adulthood. It is not related to adult hapiness (though it is related to adolescent happiness) or to happiness with any particular aspect of life. There is a slight tendency for less happy children (as they recall) to be less optimistic about life, to seek therapy more often, and to consider suicide more often. They also are less sure that life has meaning and direction for them. But all of these relationships are very weak—at most suggestive. If general happiness in childhood has substantial effects on adult happiness, we have certainly not found much evidence for it.

Nor do we see any consistent effect of a "broken home" on adulthood. Again, you might think that growing up with only one parent or going through the agony of divorce would have lasting ill effects on a child. On the other hand, one loving parent is probably better than two who are fighting with each other. Whatever the reason, having two parents who stay together does not seem to produce adults substantially different from those who had divorced parents or who were raised by foster parents.

Ah, but surely the relationship between one's parents is important. If they are warm and loving to each other, it must be better for the child and will eventually show up in the adult. Well, yes, it is much better for a child to have parents who get along well. The better the parents' relationship, the happier the child. It is not an overwhelming effect even then, but a substantial one, especially considering that we are relying on people's memories of childhood. So, the child is happier if his parents get along. And this carries over to adolescence, though with considerably weaker effect. But the effect on adult happiness? None. Let me repeat that we are dealing with small numbers of people and chancy data, but the information we have shows no effect.

Finally, we get to the one factor that almost surely must affect a child's future happiness: the relationship between the child and his parents. This has always been considered crucial by psychologists and psychoanalysts and it does seem to have effects. But even these are small. The better the relationship with either parent (the relationship with the mother is slightly more important), the happier the person is as a child and an adolescent. As adults, people who had good childhood relationships with their parents are less likely to seek therapy or to consider suicide. However, there is no overall relationship to adult happiness.

The interesting finding concerns the difference between men and women. Here, finally, Freud's ideas get some support. A basic point in psychoanalytic theory is that children are in some way especially attracted to the parent of the opposite sex. Exactly what this attraction consists of is not entirely clear. It is obviously not sexual in an adult sense. Though some people have interpreted Freud to mean that a boy literally wants to have sexual relations with his mother, Freud was much too wise to believe that even a precocious four-year-old knows about or desires sexual intercourse. But young children do want to be close to their parents, to be cuddled, caressed, stroked, and so on. According to Freud, they especially want to do this with the parent of the opposite sex. Moreover, Freud thought that children are jealous when they do not get as much attention as they want from this parent and in particular, are jealous of the other parent if he or she gets the attention they want. The young boy wants attention, physical and otherwise, from his mother, and resents his father for being in the way, for kissing and cuddling the mother. The father is a rival for the mother's affection and the boy, to some extent, is angry about this. It supposedly works the same way for the young girl, who should be relatively closer to her father than to her mother and should resent her mother.

These theories receive some support from the survey data which show that boys remember being close to their mothers and girls to their fathers. Almost 80 percent of the men said they had good relationships with their mothers while only 62 percent of the women did; conversely, 57 percent of the women were close to their fathers but only 45 percent of the men were. As I mentioned earlier, overall, children had better relationships to their mothers; but the difference between boys and girls favors the opposite-sex parent.

However, it is the relationship with the same-sex parent that turns out to influence adult happiness; and this too is what the theory would predict. The reasoning from the theory is as follows. The attachment to the opposite-sex parent is more or less automatic—almost all children are attracted to the parent of the opposite sex. The problem for children is learning how to deal with the same-sex parent, with the rival. Boys love their mothers, but have to make some kind of arrangement with their father: girls love their fathers, resent their mothers, and have trouble working that out. At the same time, it is crucial for children to resolve their conflicts with the same-sex parent for a variety of reasons. At the simplest level, a child has to get along with both parents in order to function reasonably well in the home. You may think your father is a rival, but you can't very well fight him (he is too big and, anyway, your mother won't like that), and besides he is around a lot of the time, is a powerful figure in the household, and so you have to deal with him. More profoundly, if you do not resolve this conflict, you will feel guilty about not liking your father and that is destructive. Most important, a child's relationship with the same-sex parent is a central factor in establishing sex roles. The boy "learns" to be a man, to be comfortable as a male, by feeling close to his father. If he does establish a good relationship with his father, he tends to imitate him, adopt some of his attitudes and values, copy his behavior, and generally try to be like him. Similarly, still according to Freud, the young girl learns to be a woman partly by imitating her mother. Naturally this imitation need not be total, or tied to definite, absolute sex roles. But a boy should accept his sex and a girl hers in order to be happy as adults. (Accepting one's sex does not necessarily exclude one's being homosexual. A woman can accept the fact that she is female without being sexually attracted to men; but if she does not like being female, if she wants to be male, that will almost certainly be a problem for her, whether she is homosexual or heterosexual.) That is what the theory says and much of it is broadly accepted at least in a general way.

Again, Freudian theory is consistent with the survey data: the relationship to the same-sex parent was associated with adult happiness. Men who describe their relationship with their fathers in positive terms are happier than those who had bad relationships with their fathers; and similarly, girls who had warm relationships with their mothers are happier. The relationship with the opposite-sex parent, though it was usually closer and warmer in childhood, had almost no relationship with adult happiness.

Guilt

One other characteristic of childhood seems to be related to adult happiness, namely, feelings of guilt. None of the other symptoms matters much, nor do all of them taken together. But those people who say that they often felt guilty as children are different in many ways. The guilty children had poorer relations with both parents and were less happy both as children and as adolescents. The impressive finding is that for once this childhood unhappiness carries over into adulthood. The guilty ones have all sorts of symptoms as adults. They are, as you might expect, more guilty. But they are also more likely to experience fears, anxiety, insomnia. loneliness, and feelings of worthlessness. More extremely they often feel that they can't go on, are more likely to have mental breakdowns, and to consider or even attempt suicide. Given all of this, it is not surprising that they are less optimistic about their lives and generally less happy.

Why should guilt be so strongly related to adult happiness when so few other childhood experiences are? Unfortunately, no answer can be given with any confidence. It may be that guilt is a result of poor relationship with parents or a particular kind of relationship that is not healthy, such as an unresolved dislike of the same-sex parent as described above. It may also be that guilt is a measure or general neuroticism, and all we are seeing is that neurotic children tend to become neurotic adults. There is little question that feelings of guilt are caused by strong or confused values which the child cannot live up to. If parents constantly ask too much of a child, he may feel guilty because he cannot possibly live up to their demands. Or if they make inconsistent demands—if they tell him to be sweet and well-behaved one day and criticize him for being too passive the next—he may feel guilty all the time because he is always acting wrong. This sense of always being wrong might carry over to adulthood, where he would not have a clear sense of how he should behave, and also a general tendency to feel that he is worthless.

Whatever the specific explanation, and there may well be several, childhood guilt and not getting along with the same-sex parent are two factors from early life that are closely related to adult happiness.

Adolescence

A psychiatrist who had a great deal of experience working with college students told me that all adolescents seem schizophrenic. He meant, of course, not that adolescents are schizophrenics, but that, like schizophrenics, they are uncertain who they are, have very strong conflicts, and often act one way on a particular day and entirely differently and unpredictably the next. Adolescence is a difficult and, if you will, crazy period of life. Adolescents are trying to deal with many basic problems of life at the same time. They are becoming independent from their parents, deciding what kind of persons they are, choosing a career, establishing some kind of role in life, and dealing with sexuality, its gratifications and responsibilities. It is probably because of these conflicts and pressures that, as I mentioned in the chapter on age, adults usually remember their adolescence as the least happy period in their lives. Adults recall their childhoods in quite favorable terms—about two thirds were very or moderately happy—but only half remember their adolescence as a happy time.

Presumably, a person who resolves the questions and conflicts of adolescence—decides who he is, what he wants, achieves some sort of independence, manages to get pleasure from sex without too much conflict, etc.—should become a relatively happy adult; whereas if he does not, adulthood should be difficult. We have unfortunately even less information about how adolescence affects adult happiness than we do about childhood. The little we have is related mainly to attitudes toward members of the opposite sex. This is such a central concern to adolescents that it might be expected to show major relationships with adult experience, and indeed it does, but in only limited ways.

It turns out that how well people dealt with sexuality

during adolescence is related primarily to how well they deal with it in adulthood, but not to happiness in general. In childhood, the interaction between boys and girls usually does not have a sexual element. Suddenly after puberty, people must deal with each other as sexual beings; this makes many adolescents extremely uncomfortable and awkward, while others take it in their stride. How adolescents deal with sexuality is often related to how early they reach puberty. There is a wide range of ages at which puberty occurs—from ten to fourteen for girls, eleven to sixteen for boys, and in a few cases even earlier or later than this. Because of the wide range, a sixth or seventh grade class will contain boys and girls at all stages of development. There will be some early-maturing girls who tower over the boys (in later years very few men remember that during this brief period in their lives, most of the girls were actually taller than they were—but the women remember). These girls who have reached puberty have developed breasts, their whole figures have changed, and they are becoming women. These early maturers face the difficulties of being surrounded by both boys and girls who are way behind them in development, and also of getting attention from older boys that they may not be quite ready for in terms of social development.

Even more difficulties are faced by the late maturers, who find themselves surrounded by boys and girls who are far ahead of them in development. The flat-chested girl is ridiculed or ignored; the boy who has not reached puberty tends to be much smaller than everyone else and cannot fully comprehend everyone else's sudden interest in girls and sex. These late maturers must face several years during which they cannot deal with sexuality on an equal basis with those around them.

The evidence is that those who date relatively early and who get along with those of the opposite sex have a much easier adolescence. They are happier during adolescence and this carries over into certain realms of adulthood. As adults they are less guilty, more active sexually, more satisfied with their sex lives, and happier in their love relationships than those who have difficulties in adolescence. In other words, if you do well with sexual and romantic relationships as an adolescent, you are likely also to do well with them as an adult. Not surprising, but important to note because it suggests that this particular pattern is set quite early.

In contrast, this ease of sexual relationships in adolescence is not related to other factors in adulthood; adolescent happiness in general is only slightly related to adult happiness. Again, we have very little information on this issue, but what we have implies that experiences in adolescence have little relationship to how healthy, active, satisfied, or happy one is as an adult. Once again, I consider this a hopeful result. A difficult adolescence does not doom you to unhappiness ten years later—in fact, it has little or no effect. More and more, psychologists are arguing these days that people are almost infinitely changeable. An awful seven-year-old brat may remain a brat for the rest of his life; but he may turn out to be lovely, well-behaved adolescent and a wonderfully happy adult. Anything can happen.

Nor is there any reason to believe that things are fixed at any point. As you get older and older it may be harder to change your personality or your way of dealing with the world, but it is probably not impossible. People change careers at fifty, take up painting at eighty, switch from peanut farmer to politician in middle age. They also change life styles, spouses, sexual preferences, and even actual sex long after adolescence. It should then hardly be surprising that they can change their personalities, shrug off neurotic patterns or adopt them, find a way to happiness or lose it at almost any age. People can change—that is the basic assumption of all psychotherapies. Some may need help, and no one argues that change is easy, but even Freudian psychoanalysis, which places the greatest emphasis on the childhood years, assumes that people can alter their personalities. Although our research finds some effects of childhood and adolescent experiences, the general lack of impact on adult happiness may be due mainly to the fact that people do adapt and change.

Early experiences may determine the kinds of adaptations people choose, but not necessarily how successful they are. It is possible that childhood and adolecent experiences have important effects on adult happiness that we have simply not discovered for lack of information or because the effects are extremely subtle and complex. But what we know suggests that as far as happiness is concerned, most people are not condemned to live out the consequences of childhood.

13. Faith

Chapter 10, which discussed the influence of occupation on happiness, revealed that clergymen are the happiest occupational group, followed by psychologists, artists, and entertainers. I hypothesized then that the happiness of the clergy might be related to a sense of service—of being useful, helpful, and loving toward one's fellow man. I might as well have guessed that clerical happiness came from a firm belief and trust in God, in spiritual values, and from having a strong moral code. Religion can give purpose to life and comfort in distress. Whatever happens to you happens according to God's plan; God can and does intervene in the affairs of the world; and, if all else fails, a religious person can look forward to something better in the afterlife. It certainly seems plausible that religious people—laity as well as clergy—would be happier than the irreligious.

Whatever the reasons for the happiness of the clergy, it appears that religion does not much influence the happiness of their flocks. Religion is considered an important ingredient by very few people—one of the lowest of the various factors considered. For example, exercise and physical recreation were thought to be very or moderately important to happiness by 70 percent of the people in one survey, while only 38 percent of these same people rated religion that important. This is not to deny that religion is of the utmost importance to a substantial percentage of our population, but it is a relatively small percentage.

Not only do most people consider religion rather unimportant to their happiness, but there is also little relationship between people's feelings about religion and actual happiness. Those who are religious are no happier than those who are not religious. When we asked whether religion provided satisfaction in life, we found that those who answered yes, who said that they derived happiness from religion, were slightly happier than those who did not. However, the relationship was very small compared to other factors in life. For example it is less than half the size of the relationship between happiness and love, sex, job, money, health, and so on, and ranks below almost all of the factors we asked about.

The lack of relationship between religion and happiness is even more pronounced when we consider specific aspects of religious feeling. A belief in God is part of most organized religions, and is central to all of the major Western religions. Most Americans appear to believe in some kind of God, though not necessarily a personal God who has any control of their lives. The range of belief is, however, considerable, from those who believe in a personal God who takes a personal interest in each individual and has some or even total control over everyone's life to those who believe in an impersonal God, one who perhaps started everything and plays some distant role in the course of events, but does not respond to individuals. Others are certain or almost certain that there is no God. And, of course, some are uncertain. Taken as a whole, there is no relationship between individual beliefs regarding the existence of God (and God's characteristics) and general happiness. Those who do not believe are as happy as those who do; those with an impersonal God are as happy as those with a personal one, and so on. It may well be, indeed it is almost certain, that a belief in God is a great comfort to some individuals and is central to their happiness; but apparently, this belief has little effect on others and may even interfere with some people's happiness (perhaps because of belief in God is often a source of guilt about one's own imperfect behavior or produces restrictions in one's life or whatever).

Of all the common religious beliefs, you would think that believing in an afterlife would make someone happier. If nothing else, it should reduce fear of death. Yet, we found no relationship between belief in an afterlife and general happiness. Naturally, religious people were much more likely to believe in an afterlife than nonreligious people; and those who believed in God were also likely to accept an afterlife. But thinking that there is life after death was not in any way associated with general happiness.

This is puzzling. At the very least, it should make older people, those closer to death, happier or less unhappy, but when we considered the age of the respondents we found only a slight increase in the relationship of religion to happiness as people got older. Perhaps the reason is that not everyone envisions a pleasant afterlife; those religions that make an afterlife an integral part of the faith typically offer damnation as well as paradise and it is possible that as many people fear the former as hope for the latter. Since attaining a good afterlife is usually dependent on leading a certain kind of life in this world, accepting this belief may be restricting, lead to guilt feelings and even fear of the consequences of various actions. Another explanation for the lack of relationship between belief in an afterlife and happiness is that people who believe are more likely to be miserable than nonbelievers in this world; that is, their very unhappiness is one of the factors that causes them to think that there must be a better, happier world somewhere. The belief may be some comfort to the miserable person, but he is still miserable now. The New Testament may promise that the poor will attain the kingdom of heaven, that those who mourn will be comforted; but these promises, no matter whether people believe them or not, do not make people happy in this world.

Although religious beliefs seem to have little overall relationship to happiness, there are some provocative differences among the members of the various religions in their average level of happiness. In various surveys, including our own, the happiest groups were the Unitarians and the Quakers; the next happiest were what might be termed liberal Protestants (Methodist, Presbyterian, Episcopalian). Catholics, Jews, and conservative Protestants (Fundamentalists, Baptists, etc.) were less happy and equally so. None of the differences is large, but they are consistent.

It would be a mistake to make too much of these results. It may be that religion itself has no causative effect on happiness and that the differences in happiness level are due to something else entirely. The members of the various religious groups differ in many ways other than their beliefs. For example, census data show that Unitarians are generally well educated and relatively well off financially compared to Catholics and conservative Protestants. The education and money, not the religion, may be producing the small differences in happiness we found. The differences might also be explained by cultural patterns that have little or nothing to do with religion per se. Jews, for example, have above-average incomes and educations but—if we are to believe the stereotypes found in dozens of novels and reinforced by hundreds of jokes in the repertoires of our most popular comedians— Jewish children are raised to feel guilty. We saw in Chapter 12 that childhood feelings of guilt tend to be related to unhappiness in adulthood.

In other words, it is interesting that different religious groups differ somewhat in average happiness, but the differences may be caused by factors other than the religions themselves. So many factors vary along with religion that it is almost impossible to attribute any differences in happiness simply to religious background, or to any other ethnic background.

Spiritual Values

It does not take a psychologist to say that formal religious belief is only one index of the state of what we may call the human soul. Jesus himself preached against those who observed the forms of religious life without attention to the moral and spiritual meaning behind the forms. And although wars have been fought over points of doctrine and worship, almost every clergyman would agree that spiritual values are a truer index of a person's religiousness than attendance at the church or synagogue.

By the same token, while it appears that formal religious belief has little impact on happiness, there is a strong relationship between certain spiritual values—a feeling that life has meaning and direction, confidence in one's guiding values—and happiness. Whatever their Sunday morning behavior, people are happier when they believe that life has meaning.

Consider the case of a twenty-eight-year-old single woman who works as a secretary earning a low salary, has no sex life, is not in love, but is nevertheless quite happy with almost all aspects of her life. Although not at all religious, she is confident of her guiding values and has a strong sense of meaning and direction in her life. Despite the obvious missing elements, she is optimistic that things will work out well for her. She tells us: "Right now my life is not so great because my job isn't too good, I don't have much money, and my love life is nonexistent. But I do have lots of friends and I like myself. I feel strongly that I know where I want to go and even though it isn't happening now, I'm sure it will soon. This makes me pretty happy despite everything else."

Just how she manages to be so cheerful and optimistic is unclear—maybe she has the secret of making the best of things, of enjoying whatever life offers. Whatever the reason, she focuses on her sense of meaning and direction—it is clearly a central part of her life and a key element in her happiness.

At the other extreme consider a twenty-six-year-old single male, with an active sex life, happy with his love life (though not right now in love), with a job in advertising that earns him over thirty thousand dollars. He is in good health, has good friends, and has no obvious difficulties. Only two things are missing in his life—a long-term romantic relationship and confidence in his guiding values. He does not think his life has meaning and direction. And despite everything else, he is moderately unhappy and pessimistic about the future. He says: "My life has been terrific the last few years—lots of money, women, friends, all sorts of activities and travel. My job is good and I am good at it. There is even a good future—I will probably be promoted this year and make lots more money and have freedom to do what I want. But it all seems to lack any significance for me. Where is my life leading, why am I doing what I'm doing? I have the feeling that I am being carried along without ever making any real decisions or knowing what my goals are. It's sort of like getting on a road and driving along fine, but not knowing why you chose that particular road or where it is leading."

We cannot be certain that this particular man's trouble is entirely due to a lack of values or meaning in his life, but that's the way it seems to him. For many people in a sense life has been too easy; they have never had to fight for anything or even decide anything. They drift into a particular field, do well in it, and only years later realize that they do not especially enjoy what they are doing or have any reason for doing it except to earn a living. These people sometimes express the wish that their lives had been tougher, that they had had real obstacles to overcome so that they would get more of a feeling of accomplishment. They also talk nostalgically about earlier times in history when people seemed to have more of a purpose in life, even if that purpose was simply survival. Their nostalgia is probably misguided—we know that very poor people, who do have to fight for survival on a day-to-day basis, are generally much less happy than those who can afford to pursue other interests. It is not the necessity of fighting to feed yourself that is helpful: but the sense of purpose and clear guiding values, which seem to have been more a part of society in earlier times, may indeed have produced fewer people who feel adrift. They are adrift in a sea of plenty, but adrift nonetheless.

Time after time, as we look at the statements by unhappy people who appear to have everything, we find them commenting that their lives lack meaning and direction. As usual, it is difficult to know whether lack of direction makes people unhappy or whether unhappiness makes for a lack of direction.

Yet there is evidence that points to unhappiness' being caused by a lack of a sense of meaning in life, instead of vice versa. We find—although the relationships tend to be rather weak—that people who lack meaning in their lives tend to be less happy with almost every aspect of their life. They are less satisfied with the recognition they receive, with their financial situation, their home, job, love life, sex life, marriage, friends, where they live, and even their own physical attractiveness. Given two people with equal incomes and educations, the person who feels his life has meaning is more likely to be pleased with his income. Those without a sense of meaning also are more likely to suffer from all sorts of physical and psychological symptoms. They are more anxious, more frequently feel tired, have trouble concentrating, experience guilt, have irrational fears, have crying jags, feel lonely, and sometimes feel that they cannot go on. They more often feel worthless, have more mental breakdowns, and are more likely to have considered or even attempted suicide, Much the same pattern prevails among those who lack confidence in their guiding values, a somewhat different variable, though it makes a little less difference than the meaning of life. Again, those who lack confidence tend to be less happy with most aspects of their lives and have a variety of ailments and complaints. I hesitate to make too much of this, but it does appear that spiritual values color one's feelings about reality, while a lack of them to some extent poisons or detracts from everything else.

It is worth noting that people who have a strong sense that their lives have meaning and direction tend to be slightly happier with the role religion plays in their lives and to think that religion is slightly more important to their happiness than those who think their lives lack meaning. But people who believe in God or accept an afterlife are not more likely to think their lives are meaningful. This is a surprising finding. I would have thought that one of the major effects of religious belief would be to give people a sense of direction and purpose—not necessarily particular goals, but at least a feeling that life made sense, was organized according to some rules, and that their own lives were part of a grand design. For some reason, this is not a general effect of religion. Surely many religious people feel that their beliefs provide structure and purpose and direction, but obviously other religious people, though accepting the doctrines of their religion, do not. And as far as happiness is concerned, the sense of meaning is what is important, whether or not it has a religious origin. This quasi-religious belief in meaning and direction in life is of central importance, closely related to general happiness as well as many other crucial aspects of life. For this reason, those religions that emphasize ethical values more than specific doctrine—the Unitarians and Quakers and some of the Eastern religions, which stress being good, humane, treating others well, expressing your own potentials, while downplaying the importance of a belief in God, perhaps even leaving that to each member's inclination—contain those people who describe themselves as the most happy. At this moment in our history, it seems as if personal, human values and beliefs are more closely related to happiness than beliefs concerning God, an afterlife, or sacred teachings. This is a finding that bears, after a fashion, on one of the greatest debates of Christian theology—the question whether salvation is most surely obtained through faith or through good works. I cannot speak of the world to come, but in this world, at least, good works matter more than faith.

Esoteric Beliefs—ESP and Such

Although Americans do not seem especially religious at the present time, they do have a strong tendency to search for nonmaterial things to believe in. This is shown in part by the apparent appeal of all sorts of new "religions" such as the Hare Krishna and the attraction of gurus of various persuasions. Unfortunately, we have no data on the happiness of adherents to these movements. However, this search for nonmaterial beliefs also extends to a wide variety of phenomena that are generally considered beyond normal experience and perhaps beyond scientific explanation. A remarkable number of people believe in or have actually experienced various psychic phenomena. For example, among *Psychology Today* readers 29 percent say they have experienced telepathy (reading someone's mind), and 39 percent precognition (knowing ahead of time what was going to happen in the future). In addition, 18 percent have had mystical or supernatural experiences of some kind, 26 percent had peak experiences, and a full 40 percent have felt at harmony with the universe.

Those who believe in these phenomena are neither happier nor less happy on average than those who do not believe. However, the believers do differ from nonbelievers on a variety of measures. Moreover, the believers fall into two quite different groups. First, there are those who have experienced ESP and mystical experiences. Although they say that they are as happy as anyone else, they seem to have symptoms that may contradict their statements. These people say that they had more symptoms during childhood than the average. They suffered from nightmares, upset stomachs, and so on. And as adults they are more likely than others to have symptoms such as insomnia, anxiety, and feelings of despair—symptoms that ordinarily mean the person is not doing well psychologically. This group of believers also uses drugs more often than the average person. Thus, we get a picture of those who say they have experienced telepathy, precognition, or mystical events that includes a relatively tense, anxious childhood that has carried over into adulthood. Just why these people believe in ESP is unclear. Their anxiety may cause them to seek mysterious phenomena to fall back on or to give them some excitement in life; they may be especially suggestible people who are willing to believe in things that most others will not; or perhaps they have had these mystical experiences and were so upset by them that it caused their anxiety (as a nonbeliever, I am prone to reject this last idea, but who knows). In any case, this group of believers seems generally somewhat less well off psychologically than the rest of the population.

In contrast, those who have had peak experiences and have felt in harmony with the universe tend to be somewhat better off than the rest of the population. Their health is better, and they report less anxiety, tiredness, loneliness, and less of a tendency to have crying spells. This group tells us that they used to take various drugs, experimented with many of them, but use few now—many fewer than the previous group. Again, we are uncertain why there is this relationship between peak experiences and being in good shape psychologically. Perhaps one must be happy and healthy in the first place in order to have a peak or harmonic experience (if you are upset about yourself or this world, how can you experience harmony and peace in connection with the whole universe?). Reasoning in the opposite direction, perhaps having a peak experience or feeling in harmony with the universe is so marvelous that it makes the rest of one's life seem better or actually be better. And, of course, with both the ESP experiences and the peak and harmonic ones, we have only the individual's word that he or she actually underwent it. It may be that we are dealing here with a state of mind rather than a real experience in the usual sense of the word. But whatever the explanation, we see that a great many people have these beliefs and that they are related to the general state of their lives—with the ESP group being somewhat less healthy than others, while the peak experience group are generally healthier psychologically.

Trust versus Cynicism

Although it is probably not exactly a spiritual belief in the same sense as those we have discussed earlier in this chapter, one attitude toward the world that we found to be quite important in relation to happiness was degree of trust and cynicism. Some people face the world, meet new people, encounter new situations with an open, trusting, unsuspicious attitude. They tend to take everything at face value, to assume that people are well meaning, and to look for the most positive aspects they can find. Others are the opposite—always being suspicious and cynical, looking for tricks and deceit, and focusing on the negative. There is some evidence that the trusting person enjoys life more and is generally happier than the cynical soul.

Erik Erikson, a noted psychoanalyst and theoretician, suggested some years ago that early in life people develop either basic trust in the world or mistrust. He proposed that the first year of life is critical in the development of this attitude. If the infant is treated well, has his needs met, gets warmth, food, love, and attention, he will learn that the world is a friendly place. From that time on he will have some degree of faith (what Erikson called basic trust) in everything. He will generally expect to be treated kindly, to get what he wants, to receive love, and not to have anything unexpected and bad happen to him. In contrast, if he does not get treated well, if his parents give him too little attention, if he is left to lie in his crib crying and wet, if he is hungry and has to wait too long before being fed, if he is handled roughly and without love, he will not develop this basic trust. He will always expect the worst from the world, will be suspicious, and will be on the lookout for unexpected negative events. Presumably, someone with basic trust is more likely to have an optimistic view of the world and may also tend to enjoy himself more and be happier.

We do not have any evidence that Erikson is correct regarding the time at which these attitudes develop. As we mentioned in the chapter on childhood, the connections between what happens early in life and later happiness are few and rather weak. We do know that children who are not given adequate care when they are very young tend to be less well adjusted and to have a higher rate of serious mental disturbance than others. But otherwise, there is little evidence relating this supposed basic trust to later happiness.

On the other hand, we can ask adults to tell us their attitudes toward the world. In one study we asked several questions that relate to trust and cynicism: (1) Do you agree with the statement: "I often feel like a phony or fraud"?; (2) do you agree: "Barnum was right when he said there's a sucker born every minute"?; and (3) do you agree: "I feel my life has meaning and direction"? Each of these questions has a slightly different focus, but taken together they are quite a good indication of a person's response to life. If he agrees that he feels like a phony and that people are suckers, he is more cynical and less trustful than if he disagrees. Similarly, someone who thinks life has meaning and direction tends to be less cynical and more trusting than someone who disagrees. Thus, we have some rough measure of adult cynicism.

As we would expect from Erikson's notion and from any understanding of cynicism, people who are more trusting tend to be happier. The relationship is small, but consistent. Presumably, a cynical attitude goes along with a tendency not to enjoy things, to find fault, to be suspicious, and to find less happiness in whatever befalls you.

A somewhat related question that we asked was whether the individual liked most of the people he met. This is another side of cynicism, since it applies not to life in general but only to other people. Someone who likes most people is probably more open, more trusting, and perhaps also warmer and friendlier. Again, answers to this question are related to general happiness—those who like people are also happier. And again the relationship is small.

Taken together, these four questions provide some evidence that what might be called a cynical attitude toward life and other people plays some role in happiness. Those who are cynical are less likely to be happy than those who are open and trusting. It is not a dramatic effect, but it may help account for the finding that people in seemingly similar situations vary considerably in happiness. Maybe it is their own reactions that determine how much happiness they extract from the world, and cynicism interferes with their ability to find happiness.

14. American Dreams

". . . a little house—I even know the street I'd like it to be on—with a nice garden, some guy that is tall and handsome and who loves me and whom I love, loads of kids, and dogs and cats and everything . . ."

—SURVEY RESPONSE

Many people have personal visions of the happy life. I mean not just wants, such as money or better health or a good job, but a more or less complete picture of their life style and how their world should be organized. These American dreams are by no means the same for everyone, but there are some that are so popular that they are part of our cultural heritage.

Life on the Farm

The first image consists of an idyllic life on a small farm, surrounded by beautiful country, having neighbors who are few but friendly and down-to-earth, and living off the fruits of one's own land and labor. In this peaceful setting you live with your family, which includes spouse, children, and perhaps other relatives and close friends. This tightly knit group works hard, but not too hard, is close to the earth and to the animals, has all sorts of pets running around, and naturally gets along perfectly. You are away from the cares, tensions, and artificiality of the city. You are not bothered by politics, crime, or industrial society. You earn a small but adequate living, have simple needs and wants, all of which the farm—and an occasional trip to the city—provide. Life is pure, unadorned, honest, and real. You enjoy the work even when it is hard because it is useful work that gives you food and shelter, and because it is honest work with the earth's natural elements.

People of all ages and many different backgrounds and present life situations offer this as their ideal world. One is a sixteen-year-old girl, a high school student who led a happy childhood and has enjoyed her adolescence so far, has few psychosomatic symptoms except that she worries and feels anxiety often, and has taken no drugs, does not smoke, and never gets drunk but is a "tea addict." She is happy with all of the social aspects of her life—love, friends, sex, and most other aspects as well. She says that she has experienced precognition, mystical and peak experiences, and she believes in a personal God and an afterlife. At the moment she lives in a small city. Overall she considers herself moderately happy, but she would rather live her life in a scene similar to the one described above.

"I would like to live in the country, on a farm. Live the basic life—not a nut, just easy and simple. I love horses and can't have one because we live on 3 acres—not enough. I want to be a girl who has a horse and land and I'd be happy." She adds: "I also wish I could be a better Christian, and not so much of a hypocrite."

Well, you might think this is just a young girl's fancy. She likes horses and God and wants to be out in the country communing with both of them. But consider this very similar picture of the "good life" from an entirely different woman.

She is thirty-five years old, remarried, co-owner with her husband of a small company which gives them an income of over thirty thousand dollars. She has a thirteen-year-old daughter from her first marriage, a loving, considerate, and "very brilliant" (by her description) husband. She has headaches, anxiety, feelings of loneliness, and moments of thinking she can't go on. She is only fairly happy with most social aspects of her life. She too believes in God and an afterlife and has had peak and mystical experiences. Overall she says she is very unhappy. She lives in the suburbs of a medium-size city but would like to change that.

"I would love to change lives with some farmer's wife, who works hard, works outdoors, has a hardworking but peaceful way of life. Goes to church on Sundays, gardens, works alongside her husband, and brings up her children to be stable citizens."

Here is a woman who seems to lead quite a good life—good family, loving husband, good job, friends, and so on. Yet for reasons that are not clear she is very unhappy with it all. She considers the life around her tainted by too much civilization, too much luxury and stress on material goods. So her answer is to separate herself from the industrialized, competitive society and seek peace and virtue on a farm.

Both of these people are religious, and part of their reason for preferring life on a farm is a feeling that modern life is not consistent with goodness, is somehow in conflict with their religious and spiritual beliefs. However, that is not the only reason for having this particular American dream.

Consider a twenty-nine-year-old single man with an excellent job in Chicago. He is very active sexually and socially, is involved in a relationship in which he and the woman love equally, is very happy with his love and sex lives. He has few symptoms, is not at all religious, does not believe in God, has never had mystical or peak experiences. Moreover, he is not one of those people who has everything and is still unhappy. On the contrary, he is quite happy with his life. He is very happy with the social aspects of it, with his job, financial situation, and success. He is also moderately happy with his personal growth and development. In other words, not only does everything seem fine from the outside, he also thinks it is fine from his point of view. Nevertheless, he would like to give it all up and move to the country.

"I know that I seem to have a great life. My job is good, pay very high, advancement coming. I have lots of friends, travel a lot, and have no financial worries at all. Until this year, I went out with many different women and some of them were terrific; and now I am in love with someone who is really special and she loves me. It seems perfect and in many ways it is. I can't really complain; and I do consider myself very happy in general. But I wish that instead of living in the city, I were on a farm in the country somewhere. Instead of going to a fancy office and working on stuff that doesn't mean anything just to make money for myself and for my bossess, I would rather work harder on a farm, running a tractor, feeding pigs, even shoveling shit. That would be clean work that made sense because it would be producing food for myself and other people. Also, I think life in the country is good for you. I don't mean physically, though that too. But more in terms of what it does to your sense of yourself and your values and attitudes. Here we worry a lot about other people's opinions, about pleasing your boss, about looking OK, about not getting into a fight with a neighbor or some kid on the street. On a farm, you only have to worry about doing your work and getting along with the people you love and care about. And I think that's good for you—you can be your own person. I know all of this is a little unrealistic, because running a farm is very hard, you need to know what you're doing, and I don't. I would probably go bust in a year even if I worked like a dog the whole time. But in a perfect world, that's where I would like to be and maybe one day I will be."

This man is not moved by religious feelings, or by a sense that the city is ungodly, though he does distrust motives in the city. He is, overall, quite different from the other two, yet he shares their dream almost word for word. He may be a little more intellectual about it, and also more realistic. But it is the same dream—a farm is clean, wholesome, honest; modern society is none of these. You can be your own person on a farm, but in the city you have to deal with too many other people, too much pressure, and it makes you hypocritical and distorts your values.

This is the dream. Apparently a great many Americans share all or part of it because when asked where they would most like to live, by far the greatest number choose rural areas. If they had no responsibilities or particular reasons for living in one kind of community, over 30 percent of the people would pick the rural life. To give some idea of the strength of this preference, note that the second most popular choice, the suburbs, got only 13 percent of the votes. Also, we should realize that in fact very few people live in rural areas— about 10 percent of our population. So, this is a dream, not a reality. Of course, when they say rural not everyone means life on a farm. The specific features of the dream probably vary. But it is clearly the rural life that many people want, and I would guess that the basic reasons are quite similar for everyone.

This is not the place to discuss whether people really would be happy if they managed to achieve this dream. Everyone knows that life on a farm is very hard and economically chancy, and also that modern farms are not quite so pastoral and quiet as farms used to be. The modern farmer still gets his hands awfully dirty, but at least some of the dirt is axle grease and chemical fertilizer rather than soil and manure. And it is worth remembering that rural people are not any happier, by their own self-descriptions, than people who live anywhere else, and are actually generally more pessimistic about the future than city people. Whatever the value of life on the farm, those who actually live it do not feel happier than those who live in the cities, suburbs, or towns. Thus, at least for those people who are living the dream, it is not a magical answer to finding happiness—they seem to have just about the same problems and complaints as anyone else. Perhaps the dream would work for some but it does not appear to be a general solution.

Fame and Fortune

In a sense, the opposite dream is one involving fame and fortune, and perhaps beauty. It is a monied world, a jet-set life, being recognized on the street, knowing important people, and being known and envied by all the ordinary people. This vision of paradise sometimes includes great beauty, though this is a less important element for most people—after all, if you have all the rest, you probably don't need great looks as well. Taken together, the image corresponds to the public view of many famous personalities and, indeed, many people told us that they would like to be (stop for a second—who would it be?)—Jackie Kennedy Onassis. She was mentioned more than anyone else; Robert Redford ran a strong second; Joe Namath (this was before he was traded to Los Angeles and had a bad season), and Mick Jagger followed. We have the rich and glamorous, movie stars of various kinds, athletes, clothes designers, rock-and-roll stars.

It is interesting to see just whom people mention, and especially whom they don't mention. The stars and jet set are included, but not heads of corporations, bank presidents, famous millionaires and billionaires, political figures, heads of state, Senators, leaders of political organizations, or even radical political figures. It is not power that most people want, nor influence, but fame, and especially the kind of fame associated with glamour. Thus, people want to be Jackie, but not Ari; Joe Namath, not Ted Kennedy; Jagger, not Kissinger;

Redford, not Rockefeller. There are those who do want power and influence, but it is a much smaller number than those who yearn for glamour, and it seems as if people do not believe power brings happiness, while many think that fame and fortune will.

It is somewhat difficult to understand exactly what people expect to get from this kind of life, or why they want to be the person they mention. For example, one person wrote that he wished he were Robert Redford "for obvious reasons." Other people spell out their reasons.

A twenty-six-year-old married man, a graduate student, is moderately happy with his life in general and with most specific aspects of his life—friends, love, marriage, sex, finances, and occupation. He is not satisfied with his personal growth and development or with the recognition he has received, but he has few symptoms, few complaints, and is optimistic about his future. He is not religious, lives in New York, and is considerably confident of his guiding values. He seems to be a moderately sophisticated, well-educated healthy and happy person who is doing well. And who would he like to be?

"Joe Namath because of his wealth, popularity, success with women, and success in his career. Money alone doesn't mean that much to me, but it would be nice to have it, especially if I were also attractive to lots of women and had a really good personality the way he does. It's not only that he has all of this, but life seems so easy for him. He can do and get just about anything he wants. And he always seems to be doing things that are fun. I'm not so sure about football—I don't know if I would enjoy that so much. Well, I guess I would if I were really good at it like he is. Everyone cheering for you and all. But it's that every day he can do fun things—parties, women, travelling, and all with no effort and no cares about anything except maybe whether he will hurt his knee next Sunday. It seems like a good life—exciting, fun, and everything."

Another man of thirty-seven also wanted to be a famous athlete. He wasn't sure which one—he mentioned Namath, Walt Frazier, Jack Nicklaus and Jimmy Connors. The sport did not matter; what did was the image of an outstanding professional athlete. His reasons included many of those given above, but also he thought that the athletic part of it would be especially rewarding. "In all seriousness, I can't think of anything that would give me a bigger kick than being terrific in some sport. I think I would love the crowds cheering, people stopping me on the street, and the feeling of being good at something like that, winning all the time, or even just playing really well. Maybe I would get tired of it—I guess they do and it becomes a job like anything else—but never having done it, it seems like the best way to spend ten years or so of my life."

Quite a few men voiced this dream, which is a combination of fame and wealth along with the sense of accomplishment and the fun of being good at a sport. It may seem unlikely that men in middle age, or with many years of education, or working at good jobs would fantasize about being sports figures. But they do. A great many American males, regardless of their backgrounds, seem to grow up with an image of professional sports being one of the ideal goals—obviously attained by only a few, but very desirable. They may end up being "mere" physicians, may be brilliant mathematicians or whatever, but deep in their hearts, a remarkable number hold to this dream of athletic greatness.

At the time these surveys were conducted, women did not appear to have dreams that involved athletics, though this may be changing. While the men want to be Joe DiMaggio, the women picture themselves as famous actresses. As with the men, their dream is based on money and fame, as well as looks, the ability to attract lovers, and the presumed excitement and fun of the work itself.

It is, I suppose, hardly surprising that many girls and young women have this particular dream. It is almost a part of American folklore. You are working away in a lousy job and a glamorous man walks in and orders a cup of coffee from you or buys a pair of socks, takes a long look at you, and suddenly you are having a screen test and are on your way to great success. Most of the women with this image are rather young. For example, a twenty-one-year-old woman who is living with someone and who is quite satisfied with almost all parts of her life says that she would like to be "someone like Cher Bono because she is independent, has money, confidence in herself, a lot of guys would like to go out with her and she can pick and choose." (This was before her marriage to, separation from, and reunion with Greg Allman.) "Her life just seems ideal because what she does is fun and she can do pretty much what she pleases. And she looks so wonderful, can eat as much as she wants." (The woman writing, by the way, is 5 feet 4 and weighs only 110 pounds.) "Her whole life is full of excitement with lots of freedom." A sixteen-year-old girl envies Vanessa Redgrave because "she is so beautiful, leads such an exciting life, has money, fame, men, everything." A nineteen-year-old wants to be like Catherine Deneuve for much the same reasons (the foreign actressess do very well in the popularity contest). Cicely Tyson, Jane Fonda, Marilyn Monroe (people often picked dead people as their ideals), and Mary Tyler Moore were all mentioned by women in their teens or early twenties. Presumably the actresses named would vary considerably from year to year, but the basic vision is clear.

However, it is by no means limited to young women. Just as men continue to dream of being professional athletes long past the time when it is at all possible, so many women of all ages want to be actresses. A forty-six-year-old woman, widowed, working hard for little money, unhappy with her social life, sex life, love, financial situation, and just about everything else in her life somehow describes herself as overall slightly happy. She smokes a great deal, gets drunk often, has many symptoms. Her answer, her dream, what she would like to be, is an actress. She picked Genevieve

Bujold because "she is young, extremely beautiful, graceful, talented, sensuous. She speaks more than one language, has an assured, large income, is famous, gets her pick of men, and gets invited to glamorous, interesting places all the time. Her life is fun and rewarding; she is admired by many people of both sexes."

Of course, the people chosen by both men and women are not limited to athletes or actresses. The dreams are more varied than this. Men also pick movie stars, and rock musicians, playboys (Hugh Hefner is a favorite), and other celebrities. Women occasionally mention an athlete (Billie Jean King), often list singers (Carly Simon, Helen Reddy), and, of course, Jackie Onassis more than anyone. Though sports and acting represent the prototypes for the dream of fame and fortune, each individual focuses on different aspects of it and selects his or her favorite person and field. The interesting point is that despite our supposed sophistication, this dream seems to cut across all sorts of lines, is shared by people of all kinds of backgrounds. Whatever our education, financial position, age, and whatever, many of us believe that we would be happy as a glamorous superstar of one sort or another.

One difference between men and women in terms of this glamour dream is that often women would just as soon be the spouse of a star as the star himself. No man made such a choice. Despite the impact of women's liberation, at least some women picture their ideal world in terms of whom they are married to rather than their own role—even when they are opting for glamour and fame.

Here is a twenty-one-year-old woman, unmarried, who works as a secretary earning very little money. She is a virgin, has a high school education, believes in God and an afterlife, and is optimistic about her future. She suffers from headaches, insomnia, diarrhea, and feelings of worthlessness, and she is rather unhappy about most aspects of her life and her life in general. For her the answer is:

"Linda McCartney [wife of Paul, the ex-Beatle]

because I think she is one of the luckiest women in the world today because she is married to whom I think is the most ideal man. I hope I can find a guy just like him. His music, fame, money, exciting life, everything. And his wife and family always come first. And not only is he a good father and husband and good musician, but he is good looking. I think a duplicate of him would really make me the happiest person in the world."

A thirty-one-year-old married woman with a child, who works as a teacher part-time and has a college degree, is quite happy with almost all parts of her life, especially her marriage, love life, sex life, and friends. Her biggest problems are her feeling that she does not get much recognition and is not growing and developing herself. In other words, most of the external aspects of her life are going well and she is happy with them; her concerns center on her feelings about herself, where she is going, what kind of person she is. Yet her dream is to be "Lola Redford [Robert Redford's wife]. She epitomizes to me the ideal woman—loving, caring, and supportive of her husband. While being hidden behind her husband's talent, she has established the utmost in maintaining her own identity. What greater love can be shown to a woman than a man like Robert Redford being devoted and loving to her and being faithful."

Not many women picture themselves in this way, living by their husbands' reflected glory, and feeling good because a wonderful husband doesn't leave them or have affairs. But some women do. It is hard to know whether they want to share the excitement and glamour of someone else's life (thus participating in the dream of fame and fortune) or enjoy the image of the faithful, beloved companion, tending the home fires for their glamorous mates. That dream is what we come to next.

Home and Family

Although there have been dramatic changes in traditional values in the United States over the past twenty years or so, many Americans of both sexes still have as their ideal world one of home and family. They picture themselves in a home of their own with a loving spouse, a few children (probably fewer than appeared in similar visions a generation ago), perhaps a dog or cat, and the warm glow from a fireplace. This American dream is, of course, closer to reality than the others I have mentioned because, in fact, most Americans do have families, homes and pets; whereas very few live on farms or are rich and famous. However, there has been so much criticism of this image of life, especially of the wife's role in it, that it is important to realize how many people continue to think of domesticity as the answer to their search for happiness.

As we mentioned in an early chapter, attitudes toward marriage may have changed considerably, divorce may be more and more common, but the overwhelming majority of people still do get married. None of the alternatives—remaining single, living together on a long-term basis, contract and group marriages, communes and so on—has caught on as a permanent alternative to traditional marriage, which is still the choice of just about everyone. And as we saw, married people are much happier than unmarried people. Despite divorce, despite the vast number of unhappy marriages, for most heterosexual Americans (and perhaps even for homosexuals) marriage seems to be the closest thing to a guarantee of lasting, secure, stable happiness. It should not, then, be surprising that one vision of happiness includes a loving, warm marriage; cheerful, plump children; loyal affectionate dogs; crackling fireplaces; and a comfortable home.

Probably the most interesting aspect of this dream is that it is shared by all sorts of people, young and old, men and women. It seems to cut across economic, educational, ethnic, and other lines that often divide people. The particular visions may differ somewhat:

more educated women may be more likely to picture themselves working rather than just caring for the home and family; men certainly picture themselves working; those in higher income brackets may expect maids and dishwashers; people who live in big cities may not always have a private house in their dream but instead a vast, luxurious apartment; and so on. These variations are not essential differences in the dream, which focuses on home and family as the source of happiness rather than money, fame, rural life, a good job, or anything else.

A thirty-three-year-old divorced man has a successful law practice, makes over thirty-five thousand dollars a year, and lives in a moderate-size city. He has no children, leads a very active sex life with which he is satisfied, has many friends, is not currently in love. His marriage lasted seven years and was very unhappy. At the moment, he is very or moderately happy with almost all aspects of his life except love, because he is not in love. He is very optimistic about his future, has confidence in his guiding values, believes he has a lot of control over both the good and bad things that happen to him, and likes where he lives. Overall he is moderately happy. He shares the dream.

"My life now is pretty good. I like the work I do, make plenty of money, good friends, lots of sex, and do all sorts of things that are fun. My first marriage was awful—we seemed to be in love when we got married, but it disappeared during the first year and after that we made each other miserable for six more years. I suppose I should know better, but I still think that what would make me most happy is to settle down with someone I loved and who loved me, have one or two children, and live in a nice house. If I got this, I would work less hard than I do now (I don't need all the money I make) and would spend lots of time with my wife and children. It sounds great even though I know it doesn't usually work out that way. . . ."

And a twenty-three-year-old single woman with a high school education who works as a secretary earning six thousand dollars. She has strong religious feelings, is conservative politically, has great confidence in her guiding values and in her ability to control things that happen to her. She is inactive sexually, is not happy with her social or love life, or with her job, financial situation, personal growth, or the recognition she receives. Nevertheless, she is optimistic about her future. Her vision of happiness is ". . . a little house—I even know the street I'd like it to be on—with a nice garden, some guy that is tall and handsome and who loves me and whom I love, loads of kids, and dogs and cats and everything. I don't like my job and wish I could quit and stay home and take care of everyone. . . ."

And a twenty-seven-year-old single woman, earning over twenty-five thousand dollars as a junior executive in a Chicago bank. She has a college degree plus an MA from business school, has a moderate amount of confidence in her guiding values, and feels that she has good control over her life. She is not religious, does not believe in God, has had no mystical or peak experiences, and has few symptoms except that she feels tense and anxious some of the time. She is very happy with her job, financial situation, and sex life; moderately happy with love (she is currently in love and the relationship is reciprocal), friends, personal growth, recognition, and success.

"Although I love my job and get a lot of satisfaction from it, it is not enough to make me happy. Even my friends and my lover, who is wonderful, seem to leave something missing. I think what would make me most happy is to have everything I have now, and also to have a cozy family life. It's not even that I am wild about having children—I like children a lot, but don't feel any great urge to have them. But I have a picture of a happy family with me in the middle of it—something I never had as a child—and that seems right for me. I wouldn't change anything else, I would still work hard at my job and I suppose I would have to help at home and use day care for the children. But in some way this family life would complete things for me, and, I think, make me fully happy."

And finally, a twenty-one-year-old single man, college degree, in a training program run by a major insurance company. His life and his attitudes seem quite similar to those of the woman just described. He is happy with most aspects of his life, is optimistic about his future, goes out with many women, is not in love at the moment but has been, has few friends but they are close (from high school mainly), and is not religious. He lives in a large city.

"I can see the next few years of my life very clearly in some respects. My training is going well and is mildly interesting. I expect that I will get a good position next year when the program is over, I'll make good money, move into a bigger apartment, travel more, and lead a good life. I see a lot of different women now and enjoy that, but I would like to settle down soon—not immediately but in a few years. By settle down I mean get married, have a family, buy a house in the suburbs, and take it a little easier than I do now. This may sound dull to some people, but in all honesty, it sounds better to me than running around all the time. I'm not in any hurry for this to happen, but it is what I want eventually."

This is just a sample of the people who have similar dreams. I have no idea just how many Americans share this vision, but it does seem clear that many of us from many different backgrounds and with many different characteristics see our happiness ultimately in terms of marriage and family. As I said earlier, the fact that many people with families are not happy is no reason to discard the dream; people without families are more likely to be unhappy. In other words, family life is hardly foolproof, but it may be the best chance for happiness for most people—and many people, therefore, think that there's no place like home.

Other Dreams

There are, of course, other dreams, other visions of what will bring happiness. Many people think if only they were professionals of one sort or another they would be happy. These dreamers are very specific about what they want to be—doctors, lawyers, college professors, etc.—but terribly vague about the implications Is it respect they want? or a good income? or independence? They do not say. I might add that, naturally, this dream is held only by those who are not professionals or in other high status jobs and are generally quite unfamiliar with what the work entails (and does not entail).

Then there are those who think that being marvelously talented would make them happy. They dream of playing the piano as Rubinstein does, the violin like Stern, or the guitar like Keith Richard; of being another Picasso, Michelangelo, Beethoven, or Shakespeare. Sometimes the talent is scientific and they are Nobel Prize winners in physics or medicine, new Einsteins or Pasteurs, saving the world and also having this wonderful creative genius to give them satisfaction. Whatever the particular kind of talent, the vision seems quite similar: the mere expression of the talent will give pleasure and a sense of mastery; you will be recognized as the best at what you do, and that provides respect and admiration from others; and you also give joy or some substantial gift to other people, and that is another source of happiness.

Quite a few women told us that they would be most happy if they could be like one or another of the famous women in the liberation movement. Gloria Steinem ("because she is attractive, soft-spoken and feminine, yet she is an independent woman with a challenging career who does not need marriage to be happy"), Betty Friedan, and various others were mentioned. In a similar but slightly different vein, some women named women who are not especially active in women's liberation but seem to fit the role of liberated, successful woman. Political figures such as Barbara Jordan, Elizabeth Holtzman, Margaret Chase Smith, and business figures such as Jean Nidetch and Mary Wells were named, not because of their particular fields, but because they were successful, independent women who were doing well by virtue of their own talents and personalities.

Surprisingly few people's dreams involved great power. A few said they would like to be president of the United States or General Motors in order to exercise power and influence; and others wanted vast quantities of money for the power it would give. But no one we heard from wanted to be Nelson Rockefeller or Aristotle Onassis; power was not by and large something people seemed to think important to them, or at least, not something that would provide happiness. It is possible that we have a distorted sample of people. Power-hungry people may not be sufficiently interested in happiness to fill out a questionnaire or submit to an interview. What we do know is that people who want happiness rarely think power will give it to them. That is, people do not think power *over others* will bring happiness.

Peace of Mind versus Excitement

When we consider the most common dreams, we see a reflection of the definitions of happiness that we discussed at the beginning of this book. The life-on-the-farm dream and the home-and-family dream are surely ways of attaining peace of mind. They are quiet rather than active, warm and loving and comfortable rather than sharp, sexy, and luxurious. They contrast perfectly with the dreams of fame and fortune or great talent and accomplishment. These involve excitement, fun, great activity, stimulation. In the fame-and-fortune vision there is a strong sense of sexuality rather than love, movement instead of tranquility. Thus, Americans find their answers to the riddle of happiness in different ways, presumably depending on which half of the idea of happiness is more important to them. If they want peace of mind, they envision a situation that is likely to provide it; if they want excitement, they pick a vision for that. The one dream that seems best to combine both is home and family, because it is not inconsistent with a somewhat separate life of hard work and accomplishment outside the home. In other words, some Americans picture their ideal world as composed of two separate lives—the home and the office. Home should be peaceful and loving; office can be exciting and challenging. This home-and-office solution may not always work, but many Americans think that it would. Maybe they are right. Remember that working married people are the happiest group in our society.

15. Theories of Happiness

"When one door of happiness closes, another opens; but often we look so long at the closed door that we do not see the one which has been opened for us."

—HELEN KELLER

All of the research on happiness leads to the conclusion that there is no simple formula for producing happiness. We cannot merely list a set of requirements and say that these or some proportion of these is necessary; that you will be happy if you have them, and unhappy if you do not. We do know that certain elements are very closely related to happiness. Someone who is in love and whose love is returned is considerably more likely to be happy than someone who is not in love or whose love is not returned. Married people are happier than unmarried on average; sex, good health, and above-poverty income, friends, and a job—each makes happiness easier to attain. Also, there is evidence that people who have confidence in their own guiding values, who believe that there is meaning and direction in life, and who feel that they have control over the good and bad things that happen to them are generally happier than people who do not fit these descriptions. Yet not one of these factors is either necessary or sufficient. You can have any of them and not be happy; you can lack any one of them and still be happy. Moreover, and this is the most striking finding, you can have all of them and be miserable, and there is some reason to believe that you can lack them all and manage to be happy, though this is uncommon. But we cannot provide a recipe—like a cup of love and a teaspoon of guiding values.

All of which causes us to search for some general explanation of how happiness is attained. Perhaps the reason we cannot find a recipe is that happiness depends on something more complex than a combination of ingredients, on more complicated psychological processes. To make chocolate cake you need eggs, flour, sugar, butter, chocolate, and baking powder in the right proportions; you also need to mix them in certain ways, pour them into a pan, and bake them. The ingredients alone do not guarantee a good cake. Similarly, but much more complexly, happiness may depend less on a mixture of elements than on how the individual responds to them—his or her perception, understanding, emotional reactions, and so on. Perhaps it is the psychological mechanisms of each individual that determine happiness even more than the particular experiences to which that individual is exposed.

Comparison to Others

One compelling and widely discussed theory of happiness is that it depends on comparing yourself to other people. If you are doing better than they are, you are happy; if you are doing worse, you are unhappy. There is no set level of anything—money, sex, love, whatever—that produces happiness. Rather, we look around at other people, get some idea how much of each important element they seem to have, and we are satisfied if we have about as much and delighted if we have more.

Our research provides some results that are consist-

ent with this notion. It could be argued that the effect
of money on happiness depends largely on comparisons. Very poor people are unhappy, of course, because they have less than anyone (and probably also
because it really is difficult to be very poor). But above
the poverty level, money matters little. Perhaps this is
because each group in society compares itself to similar
groups. The steelworker compares himself to other
steelworkers and other factory workers (and feels
pretty good about his income); he does not usually
compare himself to physicians or bank presidents.

The finding that college-educated people are less
happy when they earn a good income than less well
educated people who earn the same amount could be
explained in these terms. The college graduate compares
himself to other college graduates, so his income does
not seem so good—in fact, for many, it seems small. In
contrast, if the high school graduate compares himself
to other high school graduates and finds that he is
making more than most of them, he feels good about
it. It is not how much money (perhaps over a certain
minimal amount) but how it compares to what other,
similar people are earning.

Although this makes sense and, I suspect, is true
some of the time for some people, it is surely not the
whole story. For one thing, we did not find that sexual
satisfaction was related to one's notion of others' sexual
behavior. Most people think (wrongly) that others are
more sexually active than they are, but this was not
related to their sexual satisfaction or their overall happiness. Those who thought others were more active
were just about as likely to be happy themselves as
anyone else. In other words, happiness with sex depended not on number of sex partners, only somewhat on
frequency, and not at all on what you thought others
were doing. It depended on whether you were in love
and on how "good" the sex was, whatever that means.
Obviously, some people are dissatisfied with their sex
lives because they think everyone is doing all sorts of
things they aren't; but this does not seem especially important or widespread.

My guess—and this is only a guess although it is consistent with the evidence we collected—is that comparisons of this kind work for goals set by society. One's reactions to money, success in business, recognition, maybe even one's job depend largely on the values of the culture. That is, society says it is good to make money, be successful, get recognition, and have a good job; and society also defines what each of these things means. How much money is a lot? We can tell only by comparing ourselves to others similar to us. For a corporation president or star athlete, a hundred thousand a year is poor pay; for most of us, it is riches. Both evaluations are based on what other, similar people earn. The actual amount of money has almost no meaning except in relation to the person's position and what others get. Similarly, society proclaims that it is "better" to be a banker then a cop, "better" to be a cop than a garbage man. If everyone you know and grow up with goes to graduate school and is wininng all sorts of prizes in his chosen field, finishing college and getting a reasonable job is not success; if everyone you know drops out of school and works as a clerk, if at all, you are successful. Success in one group is failure in another. Recognition comes from your peers and from society.

In contrast, other crucial elements in our lives can be evaluated without comparison to others or by the definitions of society. We can experience and judge them directly. I don't much care whether Craig Claiborne or any other famous gourmet likes a particular restaurant. I may use his judgment in deciding whether to go there, but then I can taste the food for myself and if I like it, that's all that matters. Similarly, I don't need Alex Comfort or anyone else to tell me what position for sexual intercourse gives the most pleasure, though again I may use their opinions as suggestions. But then all I care about is how it feels to me and my partner. Everyone in the world may be swinging from the ceiling these days, and maybe I'll give it a try; but if I don't like it, I'll stay on the ground. Even more clearly, I know how I feel about someone I love, know the emotions, pleasures, pains, and so on myself and don't need anyone to tell me about them. And I have probably learned that I cannot decipher how happy others are in their love relationships; all too often, people who seem deliriously happy tell you the next day that they are getting divorced.

All of this seems to me to be true of most internal states that contribute to happiness. Sexual pleasure, love, satisfaction with marriage and family, as well as self-confidence, feelings of control, a sense of meaning in life—all depend mainly on the individual himself or herself, and comparisons to others are largely irrevelant.

Thus the theory that happiness depends on comparison with others is useful but far from the whole story. It probably does work for certain elements in life. It probably works for all of us at one time or another, and for certain people much more often. We do compare ourselves on some things, and do feel better (maybe even happier) when we look good in comparison, when our lives have more of something desirable than others. But there is much more to happiness than keeping up with the Joneses.

Expectations versus Achievements

A related theory is that happiness depends on the comparison between what we expect and what we get. Earlier I quoted Howard Mumford Jones's definition of happiness: "Wanting what you want, getting what you get, and hoping that the two will coincide." This is similar to the idea that happiness depends on comparison with others, because our expectations are influenced by what others get. However, the focus is different. It is a kind of self-comparison. Instead of looking around, we ask ourselves what we want (or expect) and are happy when we achieve as much, and particularly when we get more. Under these terms, what other people are doing matters only insofar as they have influenced our goals and expectations. Even if everyone makes a million dollars, we are happy because we only expected to make half a million. It is a more individualistic, internal explanation but it still argues that the actual state of affairs matters less than our personal, psychological reaction to it.

This idea is very compelling, although there is little evidence to prove it. Surely, our expectations influence how much we enjoy or appreciate any experience. If a comedy movie gets rave reviews from the critics and our friends and it turns out that we only laugh a few times and smile a few more, we are disappointed and may actually not enjoy ourselves. But if we had heard nothing about the movie ahead of time and simply wandered in on impulse, the few laughs and smiles may be enough to give us a good time. A meal that we would enjoy enormously in a local diner would be a disaster and would make us complain and be bitter and resentful in a three-star Parisian restaurant. The food tasted the same, but we expected something entirely different and our reactions, and our enjoyment, depend in part on the relationship between expectations and results. This is not just terminology. We really *did* enjoy the meal more in the local restaurant; it did make us happier. If we always got more than we expected in local diners and always got less than we expected in fancy restaurants, we would stop going to the latter even if the restaurant food was better.

I believe that this process operates in many aspects of life. Unexpected success gives pleasure and happiness; unexpected failure gives dissatisfaction and leads to unhappiness. Attaining what you expect may be more or less neutral. For example, if you confidently expect to make thirty thousand dollars by the age of thirty-five, earning that sum will give you only modest satisfaction. It is, after all, just what you expected. You may be no happier, no more satisfied than someone who expected to make fifteen thousand dollars and is earning exactly that. And it seems highly likely that you are less happy than someone who expected to make fifteen thousand dollars and is making twenty-five. He is surprised and gets a kick out of it.

Let me add that I am not talking here about dreams and fantasies that are fulfilled. If you fantasize about making a million dollars or even thirty thousand dollars but do not really even expect to earn that much, it is entirely different from truly expecting that income. When a dream is achieved, presumably that is very satisfying and may give great happiness.

Success and recognition fit this model nicely. We all have fairly firm expectations about how we will do in these realms, usually have clear expectations about what kind of job we will get and also how enjoyable the job itself will be.

I think many kinds of interpersonal, social aspects of life also are affected in part by our expectations. What do we think marriage will be like? How many friends should one have? What is it like to have a new baby? How often should you fall in love? How wonderful will it be when it happens? We all have expectations about these things, some of them reasonable, probably some of them entirely unrealistic, based on ignorance, Hollywood, and comic books. When we face reality, its relationship to our expectations is very important in determining our reactions and our eventual happiness. If we expect to have total and unleavened joy from a newborn baby, we will be very disappointed by diaper changes, three o'clock feedings, crankiness, and colic. Similarly, if we expect love and marriage to be endlessly joyful, we are in for some surprises. Unrealistic expectations may interfere with the amount of happiness babies and lovers can bring.

Even strong physical pleasure such as sex may be heightened or reduced by expectations. It is entirely possible that the thrill and delight may give less satisfaction and happiness if one expects too much. Or perhaps this applies not so much to the actual physical pleasure, but to the social aspect of sex, such as the frequency with which partners engage in intercourse. If you expect to continue having sex twice a day throughout marriage, you will usually be disappoined and may be unhappy even though you are still having lots of sex, maybe even as much as you really want. The physical pleasure is not reduced, but your satisfaction with the whole situation may be.

All of this seems eminently reasonable and I am convinced that to some extent these comparisons of expectations and achievements play an important role in producing happiness. However, we should not overstate the case. Some experiences in life are inherently more positive, pleasurable, and satisfying than others. The physical pleasure derived from sex is real and is probably enjoyable even if you expect a lot. A completed sexual act is more enjoyable than one that is incomplete, for instance, because the man is impotent. Even if both are exactly what was expected—one man is never troubled by impotence and fully expects to finish the act, the other man is always troubled and fully expects not to finish—I am fairly certain that the first man, and his partner, get more pleasure from the act than the second couple. Also, some people have very low expectations in part because they are already depressed and unhappy. They have decided for one reason or another that life is miserable and that nothing good will ever happen to them. Their expectations are so low that they are almost always reached or exceeded. Yet these people typically derive little satisfaction from this. They continue to view life as an unhappy state and occasional successes do not mean much. These may be extreme cases, but they are examples of the fact that our attitudes toward life also determine how much we enjoy what happens to us and what we achieve. If you expect misery, getting it will probably not make you very happy. If you expect to be unhealthy, unloved, and unemployed, being right will not make you less unhappy.

What You Are Used to—Adaptation Level

Adaptation is an important concept in traditional experimental psychology. All organisms tend to get accustomed to any level of stimulation they experience for long enough. This is called adaptation; and the amount of stimulation is called their "adaptation level." If you spend an hour in a dark theater, your eyes adapt to the dark, and you notice small changes from the low level of darkness. When you go out into the sun, you are almost blinded, can hardly see, and would certainly not notice a candle that was lit. After a while, you adapt to the bright light, and then again become aware of changes from that level. Some of this particular adaptation is due to physical changes in your eyes but we adapt to other things without any physical changes. We get used to the loud noise in the city, quiet in the country, the drone of our refrigerators, and after a while do not even notice them. I remember buying a digital clock-radio, taking it home, and discovering that every minute there was a loud click as the clock changed time. I thought I had made a terrible mistake and would never be able to sleep through the noise. But it took exactly one night for me to adapt so thoroughly that I never heard the noise unless I made a point of listening for it.

This kind of adaptation occurs in virtually all aspects of our lives, not just with physical stimulation. We get used to a certain level of income, a life style, a quiet or busy social life, the kind of community we live in, a certain amount of sex, the number of friends we have and how intimate we are with them, one level of recognition, a certain amount of success, the work we do, and just about everything else. And the key point of all of this is that we barely notice as long as we are at our adaptation level. Only when our lives change, when we deviate from this level, does it have a real impact. In terms of happiness, one theory is that we derive satisfaction and happiness only when we surpass our adaptation level, and unhappiness when we sink below it. Once we have adapted, only these deviations matter much.

To take a simple example that I mentioned briefly in the chapter on income, a middle-class family gets used to having a fair number of possessions. A young child may have thirty toys. She plays with most of them rarely if at all, and has a few favorites. On her birthday she gets six new toys. Temporarily, she is excited by them, plays with them a while, and soon adapts to them, loses interest in most or all of them, and now has thirty-six toys which keep her busy. In contrast, a child in a poorer family may have only six toys. He plays with all of them occasionally but probably has one or two favorites. On his birthday he gets one new toy. He is temporarily excited, plays with it a while, then adapts, and then has seven toys that will keep him busy. Is she any happier because she has more toys and received six new ones than he is with fewer toys and only one new one? Probably not. Both of them are momentarily made happy by the change—the gift—but both adapt and go back to approximately the same level of satisfaction with their toy collections. The change meant something for a while; the general level means very little.

The idea is that the same process works to some extent for all of the important elements that contribute to happiness. If we are usually perfectly healthy, any sickness makes us unhappy; but if we are usually in very poor health, a slight improvement makes us happy. If we are in a relationship with lots of love, tenderness, and sex, we are made happy by even more love, tenderness, and sex, and unhappy by less—but the usual level has relatively little effect; whereas if we are not in a relationship at all or in a terrible one, even a little love, tenderness, and sex makes us happy.

This explains why people who seem to have everything are not necessarily happy. After a while they get used to having "everything" and only getting more will have a substantial effect on their happiness. This is perhaps clearest with regards to success or money. A woman who has become the vice president of a major corporation, is earning one hundred thousand dollars a year, and is recognized as one of the most successful and talented people in the field should be happy with the amount of success, recognition, and money she is receiving. In terms of our two comparison ideas, she is making more money and has a higher position than almost any woman and practically all men, so she is doing fine in comparison with others. Also, unless she has unusually high expectations, she is probably doing fine compared to what she anticipated. Nevertheless, according to the adaptation level concept, she eventually gets accustomed to her position and income. They no longer give her a big kick or great satisfaction. At this point, only a promotion and more pay will bring excitement, satisfaction, and happiness. This is not to say that she is necessarily dissatisfied or unhappy with her position—when you adapt you simply do not pay much attention to your present level. Thus, she should not be unhappy but neither should she be happy, at least from this source.

This accounts for the endless striving of so many people. No matter how much money they make, how high their position, how much power, how much of anything they have, they want more, because once they adapt to one level, it no longer brings happiness. Nor is this limited to economic or material goods: this is not an indictment of the capitalist system. The same can apply to spiritual goals, to the search for love, friendship, sex, self-esteem, or anything (though it may be more true of material things). Someone who is inexperienced sexually may be thrilled and delighted by having sexual relations once a week. But after a while, that may not seem like enough, and he will want more in order to be happy. Someone who has no friends will be made happy when he gets one; but he may adapt to that and need more friends in order to be happy; and someone who derives happiness from faith in God or from feelings of confidence in himself or from other inner feelings may adapt to a given level of faith, confidence, or anything and need an increase in these feelings to bring happiness. This is possible, but I think the adaptation process applies more easily and forcefully to material goods, position, and other kinds of external factors. There is little evidence to support this supposition; I offer it mainly as a personal opinion supported only by our findings that material goods seem to matter less for happiness than social relationships and internal feelings.

Let me add that even though we do adapt to levels of almost anything, this does not necessarily eliminate all of the good that is derived from a particular level.

We may get used to having lots of friends and not especially get happiness from how many we have. Nevertheless, it is probably better and more satisfying to have many friends than to have few or none. We may get used to having sex five times a week and be made unhappy if we have less and perhaps happy if we have more. But I imagine we get more satisfaction from a level of five times a week than a level of once a month. And certainly it is better to be successful, get recognition, earn a decent income, and have love than not to. Or, most clearly, you may get used to being healthy or to being unhealthy, but surely the former is more likely to allow happiness than the latter.

Thus, adaptation level is not the whole answer either. I think it does provide quite a good explanation of why elements such as income make as little difference as they do, and why people with "everything" are not necessarily happy. But we must take into account some of the comparison ideas and the fact that some states are better than others. Yet, even taking all of these ideas leaves questions. In particular, why do two people who seem very similar in most respects, who have the same kinds of lives, the same level of material and social goods, and maybe even the same degree of optimism and sense of control, often differ enormously in their satisfaction with life and their happiness?

Hierarchy of Needs

Abraham Maslow, a leading humanistic psychologist, suggested some years ago that people have a hierarchy of needs that range from the most basic physiological needs to higher more humane, complex, creative ones. He believed that it is necessary to satisfy those lower on the hierarchy before one can begin satisfying the higher ones. In particular, the highest need, which he called self-actualization—a complete expression of one's potential and feeling—can be fulfilled only after all the lower ones are taken care of. Presumably, happiness comes from the satisfaction of needs.

However, the twist is that each time you satisfy one

need, a higher one comes to the fore. When you are hungry, you don't worry too much about being creative; when you are without love, you may not worry too much about expressing your need to understand the world; when you are worrying about gaining recognition and increasing your self-esteem, you may not be concerned with realizing your full potential. Thus, at each stage, almost as we discussed in terms of adaptation level, a new series of needs becomes important. Satisfying lower needs brings happiness, but then you must turn to other, more difficult needs. As long as you are hungry, that is all that matters for your happiness; once you are fed regularly, that brings little happiness and new needs must be satisfied. This means that people move up the ladder, become fuller, more actualized people, but do not necessarily become happier because they are always trying to fulfill some need and it doesn't matter too much which one it is.

Another way of looking at this is that as we ascend the ladder, as we satisfy more needs or just get more out of life, our standards and sights change. Whereas we might have been satisfied by a decent salary, some respect from peers, a person to love who loved us, regular sex, and so on, once we have all of this we alter our goals. We add requirements—having gotten all that, we want to be famous, to do something that will change the course of history, to help the world, to wield power, to be the best at something, to be creative. And if we get all of that, we might then decide that we want to be overwhelmed by religious or spiritual ecstasy, to gain full acceptance of ourselves, to express our potential fully, or whatever. Maslow suggests that we march up the ladder in a healthy, dynamic way. But it is also possible that many people are never satisfied with what they have and always ask for more, not in a healthy, self-expressive way, because we need change, or get bored, or for other unexplained reasons. Whatever the specific explanation, I think that many people do just this—constantly expand their horizons, constantly want more. In many ways this is good ("A man's reach should exceed his grasp or what's a heaven for") but it may nevertheless mean that happiness is never achieved or at least depends little on the actual level of anything you have attained. And this is why happiness is so elusive; once attained for a moment it seems to slip from one's grasp.

Talent for Happiness

Finally, there is the idea that some people have a "talent" for happiness that others lack. We all know that some people enjoy life more than others, make the most of what they have, see the world though rose-colored glasses; while others are exactly the opposite, always complaining, never seeming to experience joy, looking at the sour side of everything. And I do not here mean silly or crazy people at either extreme—not depressives who are disturbed or idiots who laugh at everything and never have profound feelings or thoughts. These aside, there are those who manage to be happy and those who do not more or less regardless of what happens to them.

I believe that such people exist and that to some extent this talent or capacity plays a role in happiness. Unfortunately, we have no evidence on what constitutes this talent or where it comes from. Our research into childhood experiences was made largely to see if we could discover the causes of adult happiness and whether certain early experiences predispose people to be happy as adults. We found a few factors that were related to adult happiness, but nothing that made a great deal of difference. Perhaps there are complex personality traits or combinations of them that allow or encourage happiness and others that do the opposite, but we do not know what they are. I do not think it is true, as some have suggested, that happiness comes from asking very little from life. Some of the happiest people have asked a lot; some of the unhappiest have asked little. Nor is there any reason to believe that true happiness comes from passively accepting whatever happens to you. Under some circumstances presumably this would help, but many of the happiest people fight constantly for what they want, accept nothing, constantly strive for more. If you accept, you may be accepting misery. I suppose it is a good idea to accept things that you cannot possibly change even if they are unpleasant; but I have seen no evidence that happiness in general depends on being passive.

In fact, having looked at a great many answers to questions concerning happiness, it seems clear that there is no one best way to respond to the world in order to attain happiness. Some seek excitement, some always ask for more of whatever they have, some are never satisfied but are very happy; others seek peace of mind and tranquillity, accept what they get, ask for little and are satisfied by almost anything, and they are very happy. This is why I called it a talent for happiness—because it cannot be defined or described in simple terms, but some people do seem to have it.

Overall, I do think the theories of happiness help a great deal in understanding the phenomenon. First, let us accept that to some extent reality is important. People have many needs and satisfying them makes it more likely that they will be happy. Complex theories notwithstanding, people who have a reasonable income, good health, love, and established long-term romantic relationship (probably married), satisfying sex, a job they like, some success and recognition are happier than those who do not. Also, those who are self-confident, have confidence in their guiding values, believe that life has meaning and direction, and that they have control over their lives are happier. Each single factor may not matter much; people can be happy without one or more and can be unhappy even with many of them; but these elements in life are clearly related to happiness.

Having said that, we should also accept the fact that a mere list of elements does not explain all there is to know about happiness. People who have everything are often not happy; people with "nothing" sometimes are; and two people who seem almost identical will differ in happiness. Part of the explanation is in terms of comparisons with other people and with each person's expectations. Similarly, if you get what you expect it may have little effect on your happiness, while if you get less, you will be unhappy and if you get more, you will be happy.

The other theories also shed light on the process. We adapt to a given level of anything—good or bad, painful or pleasurable. Once we are accustomed to it, the actual level has little relationship to happiness while deviations have. Only changes for the worse make us unhappy, only changes for the better make us happy. It matters relatively little how well we are actually doing. Similarly, once we have adapted, we may change our goals—either looking toward the satisfaction of needs higher up in the hierarchy or simply seeking more of what we have. In either case, having reached a particular level will have little lasting effect on happiness because we are now seeking higher, more difficult goals, and only these will bring happiness.

Finally, it is possible that superimposed on all of this is some personal capacity for happiness that some people have more than others. This talent enables those who have it to be happy more or less regardless of the content of their lives; those without the talent have much greater difficulty attaining happiness.

Taken together, I think these theories plus the factors outlined in the rest of the book give a fairly good picture of who is happy and perhaps what determines happiness. The major conclusion is that happiness is an enormously complex concept and feeling. No simple formulas provide a description of how to attain happiness or even how to tell if someone has it. Happiness is related to a great many elements in life, the relationships are complex, and we surely do not understand them fully. Despite the few hints discussed earlier, we know very little about the relationship between early experience and adult happiness. I remain convinced that what happens to us when we are young has profound effects on us as adults, but I do not know what the effects are regarding happiness. We do know quite a bit about the important factors in adulthood, that social factors are generally more important than economic ones, and that certain personal feelings play a major role; and we also know that the importance of each factor varies considerably from person to person. And certainly we know that our attitudes, or psychological reactions to our world, are exceedingly important to the extent that virtually identical experiences will have entirely different effects on different people depending on their responses to them.

Above all, it seems as if the quest for happiness is inevitably constant and dynamic for most people. Because happiness depends in part on comparisons with others and with our own expectations (both of which change), and because we adapt to a given state and alter our goals, we cannot capture happiness and then sit still and hope to maintain it. We change, the world changes, our needs change, and our requirements for happiness change all the time. Thus, Jefferson's pursuit of happiness is endless as long as we live. And perhaps that is for the best; otherwise, once having attained happiness, what else would there be to keep us going except fear of loss? As it is, we must continue the quest and we can hope that the search itself is rewarding.

One final thought: while it is true that happiness is elusive and that the pursuit must continue for our entire lives, it is also true that at no point is the quest hopeless. One of the clearest findings from our research is that almost nothing, except perhaps an awful, terminal illness, makes happiness impossible; and no single event in one's past makes happiness unattainable in the future. People who led very unhappy childhoods, whose parents divorced or died, who were treated coldly, who had physical and psychological problems, still manage to be happy as adults. People who have unsuccessful marriages, get divorced, and remarry are just as likely to be happy as those in a first marriage. People who are unhappy where they live and therefore move are just as likely to be happy in their new location as people who were there in the first place. And people of sixty-five and older are just as likely to be happy, perhaps even a little more likely, than younger people. The pursuit of happiness is difficult and chancy, but you are never eliminated from the game. This does not mean that everyone will find happiness; it does not mean that everyone's chances are exactly equal; but it does mean that, as far as we can tell, no matter how unhappy you are now or were in the past, you can still find happiness in the future.

Bibliography

Andrews, F. M. and Withey, S. B. *Social Indicators of Well being: Americans' Perceptions of Life Quality.* New York: Plenum, 1976.

Andrews, H. F. and Breslauer, H. J. "User satisfaction and participation: Preliminary findings from a case study of cooperative housing." Centre for Urban and Community Studies, University of Toronto, Major Report #6.

Andrews, I. R. and Henry M. M. "Management Attitudes Toward Pay." *Industrial Relations,* 1963, 3, 29–39.

Athanasiou, R., Shaver, P. and Tavris, C. "Sex" *Psychology Today,* 1970, 39–52.

Bradburn, N. M. *The Structure of Psychological Well-being.* Chicago: Aldine, 1969.

Cameron, P. "Stereotypes about generational fun and happiness vs. self-appraised fun and happiness." *Gerontologist,* 1972, 12, 120–123.

Campbell, A., Converse, P. E. and Rodgers, W. L. *The Quality of American Life: Perceptions, Evaluations, and Satisfaction.* New York: Russell Sage Foundation, 1976.

Enderlein, T. E. "Casual patterns related to post high school employment satisfaction." *Journal of Vocational Behavior,* 1975, 7, 67–80.

Fischer, C. "Urban Malaise." *Social Forces,* 1973, 52, 221–235.

Ford, R. M. *Motivation Through the Work Itself.* New York: American Management Associates, 1969.

Freedman, J. L. *Crowding and Behavior*. New York: Viking Press, 1975.

Freedman, J. L. and Shaver, P. "Happiness Survey." *Psychology Today,* October 1975.

Freud, S. *Three Essays in Sexuality*. New York: Basic Books, 1962. Original publication, 1910.

Friedan, B. *The Feminine Mystique*. New York: Norton, 1963.

Goodwin, L. "Occupational goals and satisfaction of the American work force." *Personnel Psychology,* 1969, 22, 324.

Grupp, F. W. and Richards, A. R. "Job satisfaction among states executives in the United States." *Public Personnel Management,* 1975, 4, 104–109.

Gurin, G., Veroff, J. and Feld, S. *Americans View Their Mental Health*. New York: Basic Books, 1960.

Jones, H. M. *The Pursuit of Happiness*. Cambridge, Mass.: Harvard University Press, 1953.

Magoun, F. A. *Living a Happy Life*. New York: Harpper and Row, 1960.

Maslow, A. H. *Motivation and Personality*. New York: Harper and Row, 1954.

Masters, W. H. and Johnson, V. E. *Human Sexual Response*. Boston: Little, Brown, 1966.

Mathes, E. and Kahn, A. "Physical attractiveness, happiness, neuroticism, and self-esteem." *Journal of Psychology,* 1975, 90, 27–30.

Russell, B. *The Conquest of Happiness*. London: George Allen and Unwin, 1930.

Schaie, K. W. and Strother, C. R. "A cross-sectional study of age changes in cognitive behavior." *Psychological Bulletin,* 1968, 70, 671–680.

Schultz, D. *Psychology and Industry Today*. New York: Macmillan, 1973.

Scott, E. M. *An Arena for Happiness*. Springfield, Illinois: Charles C. Thomas, 1971.

Shaver, P. and Freedman, J. L. "Your Pursuit of Happiness." *Psychology Today,* August 1976.

Srole, L. "Urbanization and mental health: some reformulations." *American Scientist,* 1972, 60, 576–583.

Streib, G. F. and Schneider, C. J. *Retirement in American Society*. Ithaca, New York: Cornell University Press, 1971.

Tatarkiewicz, W. *Analysis of Happiness*. The Hague: Polish Scientific Publishers, 1976.

Turner, A. N. and Lawrence, P. R. *Industrial Jobs and the Worker: An Investigation of Response and Task Attributes*. Boston: Harvard Graduate School of Business, 1965.

Vroom, V. H. "Industrial social psychology" in G. Lindzey and E. Aronson (Eds.) *The Handbook of Social Psychology*. Reading, Mass.: Addison-Wesley, 1969. Vol. V, 196–268.

Westoff, L. *The Second Time Around*. New York: Viking Press, 1976.

Yankelovich, D. "Turbulence in the working world: Angry workers, happy grads." *Psychology Today*, 1974, 8, 80–87.